THE NEW
CITY OF
LONDON
COOKBOOK

Best Wishes

Peter Gladwin

THE NEW CITY OF LONDON COOKBOOK

FROM TREACLE TOFFEE TO THE
LORD MAYOR'S BANQUET

PETER GLADWIN

PHOTOGRAPHY BY
SIMON WHEELER

CONTENTS

FOREWORD 6

INTRODUCTION 8

CANAPÉS 16

LARDER 36

STARTERS 54

SALADS & SIDES 76

VEGETARIAN & VEGAN 88

FISH 108

MEAT 132

EMULSIONS, INFUSIONS & GOOD GRAVY 154

DESSERTS 170

CHEESE & SAVOURIES 198

CHOCOLATES & SWEETMEATS 216

ABOUT THE AUTHOR 234

INDEX 236

FOREWORD

The office of Lord Mayor is truly unique. One of the world's oldest continually elected civic positions, the role and its responsibilities have nonetheless moved with the times. Today, the Lord Mayor is an international ambassador and key spokesperson for the UK's financial and professional services sector. As well as undertaking his or her own extensive programme of international travel, the Lord Mayor receives political, business and civic leaders from around the world on their visits to the City. In addition, the Lord Mayor also heads up the City of London Corporation, a local authority like no other. With responsibilities including the City of London Police, the Old Bailey, Epping Forest and Hampstead Heath – to name just a few – the City of London Corporation has a great variety of stakeholders. Welcoming and entertaining important people is, therefore, an important aspect of the Lord Mayor's duties.

Dinners have many uses: they can give thanks and recognition; they can encourage conversation, connection and conviviality; they can even be where business happens. Throughout the City there are Livery Halls and other historic institutions where the Lord Mayor is hosted or entertains. The highlight of the Mayoral year is the spectacular Lord Mayor's Banquet, held at Guildhall each November.

This book celebrates the culinary excellence and diversity of the City of London. The meals lovingly prepared by our first-rate chefs, like Peter Gladwin, play an important role in maintaining the City's international standing.

We are grateful that a proportion of the proceeds from the sale of this book will go to the Lord Mayor's Appeal. This charity initiative reflects the City's social purpose: each year, the Corporation partners with charitable organizations to deliver groundbreaking initiatives in and beyond the Square Mile. At the time of publication, the Lord Mayor's Appeal is working over a three-year period with three charity partners: Samaritans, Onside Youth Zones and Place2Be. Together, we are working to create 'a better city for all'.

I hope you enjoy these marvellous recipes and stories from Peter's lifelong career in the City.

Alderman Charles Bowman (pictured opposite, top left), **Lord Mayor of London 2017-2018**
Alderman Peter Estlin (pictured opposite, top centre), **Lord Mayor of London 2018–2019**
Alderman William Russell (pictured opposite, top right), **Lord Mayor Elect 2019-2020**

INTRODUCTION

Mine is a very commonplace story of a child with a particular passion turning it into a lifelong career. What might make it interesting is the fact that it has taken place in the great kitchens of the City of London. These are places that are abundant with tradition, secrets, interesting people, fine wines and good cooking.

I was brought up in an unusual household. My rather bohemian mother was the daughter of a pre-Revolution Russian artist and a Polish clockmaker, and my father was a traditionalist English Catholic whose job took him all over the world. They were an unlikely couple and life at home had a lot of quite dull routine for my sister, brother and I, but this was contrasted with the occasional excitement of hosting great family parties.

As a boy I found the anticipation, planning, preparation and then the staging of a party to be irresistible. I have always preferred all this to the socializing itself, and to this day I am never happier than working behind the scenes in a kitchen to magic up a great meal to fit a grand celebration.

One of my earliest memories was my mother allowing me to help make treacle toffee for a November 5th bonfire party in our gardens in southern Rhodesia, so that is where my story began. My first job, aged 17, was working in a Swiss hotel – in the kitchen by day and the discotheque by night with a bit of skiing in between. Combining cooking and parties seemed like a great idea and by the mid-1970s I had started my own catering business called Party Ingredients. I have always stuck to being hands-on in everything I do: cooking for the rich and famous; importing wines; running restaurants; and – together with my wife Bridget – nurturing a beautiful wine estate in West Sussex. We have brought up our three sons to embrace and celebrate everything that the kitchen and the countryside have to offer. They are now each successful in their own right as a restaurateur, a chef and a farmer.

The City of London has been a fascinating place to focus my cooking career. On the one hand there is great heritage and tradition but alongside this the City is a world business hub – multicultural, vibrant and alive with the bustle of aspiring, busy people.

In this book I want to share with you some lovely recipes that reflect the unique character of the City. They range from classical dishes to cutting-edge new creations. Alongside these are snippets of history, quirky facts and some of my personal experiences as a working chef in the Square Mile for over 40 years.

I have had the privilege to cook in magnificent places, undertake some amazing occasions and create some wonderful menus. The biggest single challenge, however, is undoubtedly the Lord Mayor's Banquet. It is the grandest annual event in the City calendar that has taken place in Guildhall for over 800 years.

Appropriately, some of the proceeds from this book are for the Lord Mayor's Charity Appeal to help the less fortunate to maximize their potential, whatever it may be.

The Chefs

Kitchens the world over are naturally diverse places. They attract all sorts of talented people from different parts of the world and contrasting cultures. Chefs trade ideas and skills, and are united in hard work and a love of the culinary arts.

Dotted through the book are guest recipes very kindly contributed by other chefs or famous people. We have adapted these to work within this City collection. The majority of the recipes come from Party Ingredients' own multinational team led by Emma Spofforth. If you see influences from South America, West Africa, Italy, the Middle East or the Indian subcontinent it is because they are all part of our ethnic mix. This is the joy of cooking.

We also have some great collaborations. Every year the Big Curry Lunch takes place in the City to support the charities of Her Majesty's Armed Forces. Here we work with a splendid team of Indian chefs from Noon Foods and we have the Army Catering Corps chefs on the front line. Some images from this year's event can be seen on pages 68–69.

Another splendid occasion was a banquet hosted in Guildhall by the People's Republic of China. A huge team of non-English speaking Chinese chefs were supplied to supposedly work under my direction, but once let loose they became a complete law unto themselves. Shouting instructions to one another in many different dialects, food flying across surfaces, woks bursting into flames and differing dishes being dispatched in all directions – it could have been midtown Shanghai.

From all these experiences we learn new things and our world food exploration is expanded.

The Places

I have cooked in many wonderful historic locations throughout this country and beyond – palaces, private estates, fields or forests and even in the great kitchens of Windsor Castle (but some of these tales are for another book). It is a very special experience to pick herbs in the kitchen garden of a stately home to garnish a dish for his Lordship's table, or to walk through noble rooms and galleries after all guests have departed and just soak in the atmosphere of dinners past.

There is a great tradition of fine dining rooms in the City of London – from Mansion House, where the Lord Mayor resides for his year of office; to the Guildhall, which has been the seat of local government since 1440; to the many Livery Halls of the City.

The Livery Halls are often hidden behind ancient gateways or within discrete courtyards. They are the homes of Livery Companies, which are each based around a craft, trade or profession. Some date back to the 11th century.

There is much more to the Livery Companies than just dining. They remain relevant and extremely active today, taking responsibility for the governance and development of their heritage. For example, The Goldsmiths' Company is responsible for the testing of gold, silver and other precious metals, as well as supporting and sponsoring the jewellery trade. The Butchers' Company is involved in the management of Smithfield Market and the Apothecaries' Society award postgraduate medical qualifications.

Other Companies, such as the Merchant Taylors, Haberdashers and Skinners, run education trusts, charities and almshouses. New Livery Companies are still being formed – for example, the Information Technologists, Security Professionals and Environmental Cleaners – each with a role to play in steering a secure future for their industry.

Every Livery Hall has its own character and charm. Some are very grand and palatial (for example, the Drapers or Fishmongers); others are rather mystical with dark wood panelling and work by candlelight (such as the Armourers & Brasiers or the Tallow Chandlers). Some have the atmosphere of a fine country house (the Skinners or the Apothecaries). Only 37 of the Livery Companies now have their own Halls, so others are itinerant.

There are several Livery Halls whose trade relates to food: the Bakers, the Butchers, the Farmers, the Fishmongers and the Grocers; and to satisfy our thirst there are the Brewers and the Vintners. All the Halls have a great tradition of hospitality and many are available to hire for business and private entertaining.

The Occasions

I am going to begin by showing off a little. Some of the most special occasions that I cook for are small exclusive dinners in the City where the food is there to complement the very finest wines. The Chef must, of course, sample both sides of the pairings.

King scallops with a vanilla butter must be pitched just right to serve with a 2014 Corton-Charlemagne; a saddle of English rose veal with wild mushrooms to grace a 1988 Lafite Rothschild; or a Stilton Soufflé that can do justice to the 1996 Penfolds Grange; even a Tarte Tatin to partner the legendary 2001 Château d'Yquem. One day my own Nutbourne Sussex Reserve might be named in a list like this as the perfect complement to English asparagus, but I wouldn't like to be too presumptuous.

The City has a long tradition of hosting great Royal occasions within Guildhall, often following a service of thanksgiving at St Paul's Cathedral. I have had the honour of cooking for the Queen Mother's 100th Birthday, both the Queen's Golden and Diamond Jubilees and Her Majesty's 90th Birthday commemoration. These great national celebrations call for elegant simplicity using the very best British ingredients. All the suppliers, chefs and service teams get a tremendous thrill out of being a part of these historic occasions.

CORPORATION OF LONDON

Luncheon
in celebration of the
Golden Jubilee
of
Her Majesty Queen Elizabeth II

GUILDHALL
Tuesday, 4th June 2002

EⅡR

The Right Honourable the Lord Mayor
MR. ALDERMAN MICHAEL OLIVER

Sheriffs
MR. ALDERMAN MICHAEL SAVORY
DAVID MAULEVERER, ESQ.

Chairman of the City Lands and Bridge House Estates
JONATHAN CHARKHAM, ESQ, CC, Chief Comm

MENU

Bouquet of Asparagus
Ribbons of Scottish Smoked Salmon
Sancerre, Domaine de la Moussière, Mellot 2000

★★★

Tournedos of Beef
Golden Soufflé of Globe Artichoke
Sage Butter Sauce
Jersey Royal New Potatoes
French Beans
Château Léoville Barton 1989

★★★

Meringue Vacherin
Pearls of Passion Fruit
Raspberry and Spiced Orange Ice Cream
Brown Brothers Family Reserve,
Noble Riesling Kings Valley 1997

★★★

Coffee
Petits Fours
Dalwhinnie 15 year old

The City also hosts a very grand and formal State Banquet when a visiting Head of State comes to the UK for an official state visit. We have been fortunate enough to cater for many of these over the years and each one presents its own set of challenges. The President of Turkey brought his own food taster to avoid poisoning; the President of Italy had an aversion to anything not from Italy; the Emperor of Japan needed dishes that were lean and light and the King of Spain did not do dairy. The President of France made a point of arriving late and leaving early (difficult when dinner is for 700 guests and timed to the last second) – and Bill Clinton insisted on drinking Coca-Cola. He was served by my son Richard, who thought he was very cool – Bill winked and said that he did not need it in a glass.

A lifetime of cooking for very special occasions has been a great privilege and not one many chefs have been lucky enough to have.

The Cooking

A lot has changed in the 40-plus years that I have been involved in the City – tastes, diets and styles come and go but the core values of delicious food and warm hospitality have remained constant. Fine cuisine is an evolution, not an invention, and what was the height of fashion in one decade is often discarded in the next but then reinvented in a new guise a few years later.

The history of banqueting and fine dining in the City goes back centuries. Records show that in 1555 the Mayor and Sheriffs were granted the sum of £100 from the City coffers to put on a 'Great and Sumptuous Feast'– the menu is not known.

Nearly eighty years later, for the 1634 Lord Mayor's Banquet, there is a well-documented bill of fare to include: 'pullets, pheasants, partridges, larks, swan, turkey, hare, capon, carp, venison pasty, cold tongue pie, fresh salmons, lobsters, jelly, oringadoe pie, almond leach, preserved tart and marzipan'.

By the 18th century a very set protocol for fine dining had been established. Up to 25 different dishes of soups, meats, fishes, vegetables and accompaniments would be laid out on the dining tables for guests to pass and help themselves. When all had had their fill, a similar number of pastries and lighter dishes would be presented. Then there would be a final course of dried fruits, small cakes, nuts and sweetmeats.

By the Victorian era multiple courses, known as removes, came into play. A banquet would begin with a clear turtle soup; there would be fish courses, game courses, roast meats, salads and, of course, puddings, jellies, blancmanges and ices. Up to 12 courses would be expected for a serious dinner.

Something clearly went wrong during the depressed years of war in the 20th century and when I began catering in the 1970s it was with a firm conviction that we could and would do better than prawn cocktail, roast beef and spotted dick. Having worked in Switzerland and France, I was convinced of the potential.

I remember my first pitch for a City banquet – at the time these grand events were more about ceremony, service and glamour than the actual food on the plate. The selection committee was not used to chefs coming out from the kitchen and when I said that I wanted to just talk about the food they were aghast. But we won the day and I was appointed to undertake my first Lord Mayor's banquet.

I believe that day made a lasting change at the City Corporation – it was an 'emperor's new clothes' moment. From then on food has been the focus; whether it was my old friend Anton Mossiman, Charles Boyd or Mark Groves catering for an event.

The decade of Nouvelle Cuisine was nothing to be proud of: big on presentation, small on portion, generous in hype. This in turn developed into the 'wow factor', with every dish needing to meet the criteria of being a visual sensation.

Today we have a much more worthwhile culinary period focused on sustainability, seasonality and healthy eating. There are many more requirements for vegan, vegetarian or pescatarian diets, and every diner is more conscious of what they are eating. The food should be creative and diverse but must also be understandable, healthy and not harmful to the planet we live on.

The Menus

I am often asked for advice on how best to plan a good menu. There are no set rules; we don't need menu protocols but it is all about balance.

An eminent physician named Sir Francis Avery Jones was a neighbour of ours. He told me that in a good diet you can eat anything you wish to in moderation; just make sure it is properly balanced with eating things that are good for you.

A great menu should surprise, delight and satisfy all at the same time. Here is a checklist for planning your own:

• Seasonality. Use the best ingredients of the season – they will always taste better.

• Choose your personal favourites and dishes you believe your guests will enjoy.

• Be ambitious and adventurous. There are thousands of wonderful culinary delights from around the globe waiting for your discovery.

• Contrast flavours and textures but make sure one dish does not overwhelm the next.

• Offset any heavy dishes with lighter ones.

• Think about colour and visual presentation. We eat with our mouths but feast with our eyes.

• Carefully choose wines to complement the food. Wine and food must never compete for attention and the combination should exceed the sum of the two.

• Finally, by all means use a recipe book but use your own experience, taste and talent to make every dish your own.

From the great traditions of the City to the multicultural approach of today, the more we learn about the cooking, the more interesting and magical the Square Mile becomes. So let us begin our culinary tour along alleyways with peculiar names, through hidden doorways and into the kitchens of the City of London, to see what recipes we discover.

Peter Gladwin

CANAPÉS

CHARGRILLED COURGETTE CANNELLONI WITH BEETROOT, ORANGE & COBNUTS

I tell my kitchen team that the three essential elements for a canapé are visual delight, an easy-to-eat single bite and a delicious explosion of flavour in the mouth. This is a lovely canapé – vibrant colours, full of flavour and delectable!

MAKES APPROX. 20

Ingredients

5 courgettes

100g peeled, cooked beetroot

200g cream cheese

zest of ½ orange

1 tsp red wine vinegar

salt and black pepper

50g cobnuts or hazelnuts, roasted and roughly chopped, to garnish

Equipment

wide-mouth peeler

ribbed griddle pan

• Using the wide-mouth peeler, slice the courgettes lengthways into thin long strips.

• Heat a dry griddle pan over a high heat. Chargrill the courgette strips for 2–3 minutes on one side only.

• Blitz the cooked beetroot in a food processor to make a smooth purée.

• Mix together the cream cheese, three-quarters of the orange zest and red wine vinegar to make a thick paste. Season to taste with salt and pepper.

• Curl the courgette strips into a cylinder (keeping the chargrill marks on the outside).

• Place the courgette strips upright on a serving platter, pipe in the beetroot purée and garnish with the roughly chopped nuts and the remaining orange zest.

'There is no sincerer love than the love of food.'
George Bernard Shaw

SWEET POTATO RÖSTI WITH CRISPY PANCETTA

Too many canapés are based around gluten, such as a small toast or a pastry case. Today there are so many special dietary requirements to cater for that we have to think about alternatives. These mini rösti are something quite different: a delicious sweet/savoury potato mouthful topped with sour cream and crispy bacon. Try making a larger version as a terrific breakfast dish.

MAKES 20

• Grate both types of potatoes using a box grater. Sprinkle with the salt and leave for 15 minutes for the liquid to be drawn out.

• Drain well and squeeze in a tea towel to remove as much moisture as possible.

• Combine the grated potato, spring onions, honey and pepper in a mixing bowl.

• Lay the pancetta on a baking sheet between two sheets of baking paper (this is a great tip for keeping bacon flat).

• Cook the pancetta in a preheated oven at 200°C/gas mark 7 for 10 minutes until crispy. Allow to cool, then break into shards.

• Shape the potato mixture into 20 little balls, then slightly flatten.

• Heat some of the butter in a large frying pan over a moderate heat. Fry the balls in batches in the hot butter (for approximately 2–3 minutes) until golden on all sides.

• Remove from the pan and drain on kitchen paper while you fry the rest in the remaining butter.

• Reheat when required in a moderate oven (180°C/gas mark 6) for approximately 5 minutes.

• Just before serving, pipe a blob of sour cream onto each rösti, stick in a pancetta shard and finish with the reserved greens of the spring onion.

Ingredients

2 sweet potatoes, peeled

1 waxy potato, peeled

2 tsp rock salt

2 spring onions, finely chopped, reserving some of the green ends for garnish

2 tsp runny honey

2 tsp black pepper

5 slices smoked pancetta

80g unsalted butter (this can be substituted with oil, but butter adds richness)

2 tbsp sour cream

COOKS' COMPANY

The Cooks' Company is one of the oldest Livery Companies in the City of London. Incorporated by Royal Charter in 1482, its origins can be traced back to around 1170 with the joining of two medieval guilds of cooks – the Cooks of Eastcheap and the Cooks of Bread Street. It is the smallest of the London Liveries and is limited to 75 Liverymen by Royal Charter.

The Cooks' Company is the only Livery Company to have two Masters. The most likely explanation for this is that this was a pragmatic solution devised when the King and the Lord Mayor both wanted a banquet on the same night and obviously both wanted it prepared by the Master Cook.

BUTTERNUT & THYME TARTE TATIN

A tarte Tatin is basically a caramelized tart cooked upside down and then served turned over the other way. It was apparently first created by accident by two sisters named Tatin, who ran a small hotel of the same name near Orléans in central France. It is traditionally made with apple but can be adapted for all sorts of fruits or vegetables. These mini Tatins are satisfying to make, and can be produced well in advance or even frozen until needed.

MAKES 20

Ingredients

2 butternut squash, peeled

1 x 320g sheet ready-rolled puff pastry

100g caster sugar

1 tsp red wine vinegar

1 tsp thyme, finely chopped, plus sprigs to garnish

salt and black pepper

a little oil, for oiling

Equipment

4cm and 5cm pastry cutters

20 x 4cm-indent bun baking tray

• Cut the butternut squash crossways into 5mm thick slices. Using the 4cm pastry cutter, stamp out 20 small butternut discs from the slices. Cook the offcuts for use in a salad or soup.

• Roll out the pastry on a floured work surface. Using the 5cm cutter, cut out 20 circles of puff pastry.

• Heat the sugar in a small pan over a low heat and allow to melt and caramelize to a deep golden colour.

• Take the pan off the heat and add the vinegar – but stand well back as it will splutter.

• Add the chopped thyme and season with salt and pepper.

• Oil the bun tray then carefully spoon a little of the caramel mixture into the bottom of each indent. Place the butternut slices on top of the caramel. Cover with the puff pastry discs, tucking them in around the edges.

• Bake in a preheated oven at 180°C/gas mark 6 for 12–15 minutes until golden brown. Allow to cool for 5 minutes before using a small round-ended knife to turn the little tarts out and over.

• Reheat before serving, garnished with the reserved thyme sprigs.

'I can't stand people that do not take food seriously.'
Oscar Wilde

RABBIT BONBONS WITH RED GOOSEBERRY COMPOTE

Please don't be put off by the idea of eating rabbit. It is delicious, lean, sustainable meat from the English countryside with a good subtle flavour – and loads of potential in the kitchen. These small bonbons are made with the addition of pork sausage meat to increase the fat content and help them to bind. The red gooseberry compote is a great accompaniment but, depending on the season, this can be substituted for a cranberry relish, our Fennel & Kumquat Marmalade (see page 52) or a Dijon mustard mayonnaise.

MAKES 20

- Fry the onion in a little oil in a heavy-based pan over a moderate heat for 6–8 minutes without allowing it to colour. Leave to cool.

- Place the rabbit meat, sausage meat, sage, fried onion, nutmeg, pepper and salt in a food processor and combine.

- Divide the mixture into 20 pieces and roll into even-sized balls in the palms of your hands.

- Place the flour in a flat dish with a little salt and pepper and roll the balls in the flour until lightly covered. Dip the meatballs into the beaten egg and then roll in the breadcrumbs until fully coated.

- In a heavy-based frying pan over a moderate heat, fry the balls for 4–5 minutes until golden brown. Allow to cool.

- To make the compote, place the gooseberries, onion, lime, sugar and vinegar in a small pan over a low heat. Gently simmer until the liquid has reduced and you have a jammy consistency. Season to taste with salt and pepper.

- Neatly spoon small mounds of the compote onto individual dishes or a serving platter.

- Reheat the bonbons in a preheated oven at 180°C/gas mark 6 for 6 minutes, just before serving, then skewer them individually on top of the compote. The idea is that guests can scoop up the tasty gooseberry compote with the rabbit. Add the chervil sprigs, to garnish.

Ingredients

1 small onion, finely diced

500g rabbit meat

150g sausage meat

5 sage leaves, shredded

grated nutmeg

50g plain flour

2 eggs, lightly beaten

200g fresh breadcrumbs

salt and black pepper

oil, for frying

For the compote

300g red (or green) gooseberries

1 onion, finely diced

1 lime, juice and zest

2 tbsp caster sugar

2 tbsp white wine vinegar

chervil sprigs, chopped, to garnish

DICK WHITTINGTON

We have all heard of the Dick Whittington from pantomimes – a humble boy from Gloucestershire who, together with his cat, walked to London to seek his fortune. He met the beautiful daughter of a rich merchant, then eventually made his fortune, married the girl and became Lord Mayor of London three times. But in reality, Sir Richard Whittington was born in the late 1350s – a nobleman from Gloucestershire who came to London to become a Mercer (trading in valuable silks and cloths). He served as Lord Mayor in 1397, 1406 and 1419. When he died in 1423, he left his fortune to establish almshouses, a college, a library and sanitation for the poor of the City. Whichever version you prefer, he was quite a role model for all the Lord Mayors that followed.

GREEN HERB MACARONS WITH GOAT'S CHEESE

Macarons give scope for lovely sweet/savoury combinations and this recipe balances the sweetness of a herby almond meringue with the savoury of goat's cheese and the aromatic flavour of Thai basil. We are using a micro cress to finish off the presentation of the canapé. Of course this is not essential, but if you have a good supplier or even grow your own micro herbs, they will just add to the visual impact.

MAKES 20

Ingredients

2 sprigs of chervil

6 tarragon leaves

Thai basil leaves, 2 for drying, the rest shredded for garnish

50g icing sugar

100g ground almonds

2 large eggs, separated

80g caster sugar

pinch of salt

shiso cress, to garnish

For the filling

120g soft goat's cheese

a dash of milk

black pepper

Equipment

dehydrator or airing cupboard

piping bag set

- Begin by drying the herbs. Lay out the herb leaves on greaseproof paper and place them either in a dehydrator or an old-fashioned warm airing cupboard overnight.

- Line one or two baking trays with baking paper.

- Place the icing sugar, ground almonds and herbs in a liquidizer or food processor and blitz until they are perfectly blended. Now rub this mixture through a sieve.

- Whisk the egg whites in a bowl until they form soft peaks. Add the caster sugar, a teaspoon at a time, while continuing to whisk. Once all the caster sugar has been incorporated, add a pinch of salt and continue to whisk for a further 5 minutes.

- Gently fold in the sieved almond mixture. Transfer the meringue to a piping bag and pipe 3cm mounds onto the prepared baking trays, spacing them apart.

- Tap the tray on the work surface several times to settle the macarons, then set aside to stand at room temperature for 15 minutes.

- Bake the macarons in a preheated oven at 150°C/gas mark 4 for 10 minutes until crisp on the outside but still soft in the centre. Transfer to a wire rack to cool.

- To make the filling, blend the goat's cheese with a dash of milk and plenty of pepper in a bowl until it is a smooth, soft consistency.

- Transfer the mixture to another piping bag and use it to sandwich the macarons together in pairs.

- Finish with the shredded Thai basil and shiso cress.

A CHEF'S TOQUE

A toque (or toque blanche) is the tall, starched white hat worn by chefs to keep hair out of food. The toque comes in many shapes and sizes and, by tradition, the taller the hat, the more senior the chef.

The grandest hats are also pleated – supposedly a pleat for every culinary skill mastered. One hundred pleats denotes the chef's ability to prepare an egg 100 ways.

HORSERADISH & ROSEMARY SCONES WITH CHANTERELLE MUSHROOMS

A freshly baked homemade scone is a wonderful thing. Make sure you have a few spares for any family members around when you are baking. As with a lot of my baking and pastry advice, the important thing here is a light touch so that you do not overwork the dough and make it chewy.

MAKES APPROX. 20

Ingredients

225g plain flour, plus extra for dusting

2 tsp baking powder

1 tsp salt

55g salted butter, chilled

150g Cheddar cheese, grated

150ml milk, plus extra for brushing

1 tbsp freshly grated horseradish

2 fresh rosemary sprigs, 1 sprig with leaves removed and finely chopped, the other for garnish

red amaranth cress, not essential, but nice

For the topping

100g fresh chanterelle mushrooms

a little butter, for frying

2 tbsp horseradish cream

Equipment

3cm pastry cutter

• Sift the flour, baking powder and salt into a mixing bowl. Cut the butter into small knobs, add it to the flour and rub it in with your fingertips until the mixture resembles breadcrumbs. Mix in the grated cheese.

• Using a small palette knife, make a well in the centre of the mixture and pour in the milk and horseradish. 'Chop' the mixture with the knife to blend it until it comes together in a ball.

• Turn the dough out onto a floured work surface, knead lightly, and then roll it out to a thickness of 3cm. Stamp out 3cm rounds using a pastry cutter.

• Place the scones on a lined baking tray, spacing them apart. Brush the tops with a dash of milk and sprinkle over some chopped rosemary. Bake in a preheated oven at 190°C/gas mark 7 for 12–15 minutes until risen and golden.

• Meanwhile, lightly fry the chanterelles with a little butter in a small pan over a moderate heat.

• Cut the scones in half. Top each half with a pile of mushrooms and a dollop of horseradish cream

• Finish each scone with a rosemary leaf and red amaranth cress. Serve warm.

ASPARAGUS SPEARS WITH SZECHUAN PEPPERCORNS

By definition, a canapé is a pre-dinner snack comprising of something savoury presented on a croûte or small round of pastry. The actual word apparently refers to a sofa on which you might delicately perch while partaking in pre-dinner refreshments. Spears of asparagus definitely don't qualify as an authentic canapé, but it is lovely to have something very simple and fresh as an appetizer.

MAKES 20

• Cut the asparagus into even 10cm lengths (we will just use the tips but do save the rest for stock or soup).

• In a medium-sized pan of boiling water, blanch the asparagus for just 3 minutes.

• Drain and dry the asparagus, then drizzle with olive oil.

• Place the griddle pan over a high heat to become very hot then sear the asparagus spears for 2–3 minutes on it. Press them down well to get good black rib marks.

• Arrange the spears on a platter and finish with a sprinkle of peppercorns and rock salt. It is as simple as that.

Ingredients

20 asparagus spears

a little olive oil, for drizzling

Szechuan peppercorns and rock salt

Equipment

ribbed griddle pan, preferable, but not essential

ENGLISH BACCHUS

Bacchus is England's answer to New Zealand Sauvignon Blanc; it is green and grassy with a hint of summer elderflower. It is great as a refreshing aperitif, but also a good food wine that can be paired with anything from white fish to barbecued pork. It is also a perfect marriage with English asparagus.

I run a small group of London restaurants, but my brothers and I were brought up at Nutbourne Vineyards in West Sussex. We have had our fair share of the year-round activities, challenges and excitement of the annual harvest. In the past 30 years the wine industry in this country has expanded from production of under 2 million bottles to the great bumper harvest of 2018 producing 15.6 million bottles. The focus is on traditional-method sparkling wines, but the still whites are refreshingly crisp and floral. There is not another element of farming in the UK with such dynamic momentum.

Bacchus wine is produced from Norfolk to Cornwall and has different flavour profiles as it goes. I am very pleased to say that our family vineyard won the President's Trophy for the best Bacchus grown in the UK at the Wines of Great Britain Awards, 2018.

Richard Gladwin,
Restaurateur and Wine Blogger

DILL BLINIS WITH SMOKED SALMON, CRÈME FRAÎCHE & CAVIAR

A timeless classic canapé that will always go down a treat, whether entertaining High Court judges from the Old Bailey or hosting a celebration with teenage children. I recommend you make more blinis than you think you need – they always seem to disappear.

MAKES APPROX. 20

- In a bowl, mix together the flour, bicarbonate of soda, cream of tartar, sugar and salt.

- In a separate bowl, mix the egg and milk. Add to the dry ingredients and blend together. Add the chopped dill.

- Heat a small amount of oil in a heavy-based frying pan over a moderate heat. When the oil is hot, wipe it off with some kitchen paper. Using a teaspoon, drop individual rounds of the mixture into the pan. The rounds will spread a little.

- After a minute or so bubbles will form and then burst. As they burst, flip the blinis over using a palette knife and cook the other side. Remove from the pan and set aside to cool on a wire rack.

- Spread a little crème fraîche on each blini and place a neatly folded strip of smoked salmon on top.

- Add a small dollop of crème fraîche, a few caviar eggs from the jar and a tiny sprig of dill to decorate each blini.

- Arrange on a stylish platter and store in the fridge until ready to serve with oodles of Champagne.

Ingredients

100g plain flour

1 tsp bicarbonate of soda

1 tsp cream of tartar

25g caster sugar

pinch of salt

1 egg

150ml milk

2 tsp dill, finely chopped, plus sprigs to garnish

a little oil, for frying

For the topping

500g smoked salmon, cut into small strips

250ml crème fraîche

small jar of black caviar

'I drink it when I am happy, and when I am sad. Sometimes I drink it when I am alone. When I have company I consider it obligatory. I trifle with it if I am not hungry, and drink it when I am. Otherwise I never touch it – unless I am thirsty.'
Madame Lily Bollinger

FILO TULIPS WITH OXFORD BLUE, ELDERBERRY & LESSER CELANDINE

From a chef's point of view, a great banquet in the City is often preferable to a large-scale canapé party. We allow 14 bites per person for a full-length reception. If there are 800 guests that is 11,200 items to individually prepare. Even at home, canapé production can be a daunting task if each one is to be pretty and perfect. These little Filo Tulips include foraged elderberries and lesser celandine, but you can use finely diced commercially produced blueberries and watercress instead.

MAKES APPROX. 20

Ingredients

2 sheets filo pastry

20g butter, for greasing

100g Oxford Blue cheese

a little milk

20g elderberries

salt and black pepper

small bunch of lesser celandine, finely shredded

Equipment

ruler

20 x 4cm-indent bun baking tray

• Lay the two sheets of filo flat on a surface and, using a ruler, carefully cut into 5cm squares. Place two squares together to form a star shape.

• Melt the butter in a small pan over a low heat, brush the baking tray indents with butter, lay the pastry stars inside and brush with a little more butter.

• Bake in a preheated oven at 180°C/gas mark 6 for 5 minutes. Set aside to cool on a wire rack.

• In a small mixing bowl, blend the blue cheese with a little milk using an electric hand whisk to mix to a smooth consistency. Season well with salt and pepper.

• Spoon the cheese into the filo cases, then top with the elderberries and shredded lesser celandine.

• Keep in the fridge until ready to serve.

OLIVE BARK TUILES WITH PESTO & HERITAGE TOMATO

This is such an elegant and stylish canapé, it will be well worth mastering the art of the tuile. The only downside is that the final assembly must be carried out at the last minute or the tuile will go soggy before it can be enjoyed.

MAKES APPROX. 20

- Blitz the olives in a food processor, then lay them out on a baking sheet.

- Dry in the oven on a very low heat or in a dehydrator for several hours. When ready, grind the dried olives to a fine powder using a pestle and mortar.

- Melt the butter and glucose together in a small pan over a low heat, take off the heat and add the flour and egg whites. Stir in the olive powder and chill for 30 minutes.

- Line a flat baking sheet with baking paper and place your template on top. Using a small palette knife, spread a thin layer of the mixture across the template. Lift off, leaving perfect rectangles on the sheet.

- Bake in a preheated oven at 180°C/gas mark 6 for 5 minutes. Now this is the tricky bit! Allow to briefly cool but while still warm and flexible, lay each tuile lengthways over the handle of a wooden spoon and allow to get the curved effect of a piece of bark.

- Make the nasturtium pesto by placing the nasturtium leaves, pine nuts and garlic in a blender with the olive oil to make a thin paste. Reserve a little of this thin paste to drizzle on the finished canapé and combine the rest with the cream cheese. Season to taste with salt and pepper.

- To finish, pipe nasturtium pesto along the length of your tuile, top with a sprinkling of tomatoes and a drizzle of the thin paste. Serve immediately.

Ingredients

60g black olives

50g salted butter

36g glucose syrup

42g plain flour

42g egg white

For the topping

12 nasturtium leaves or flowers

40g pine nuts

1 small garlic clove

50ml olive oil

200g cream cheese, softened

salt and black pepper

3 multicoloured heritage tomatoes, deseeded and finely cut

Equipment

dehydrator (optional)

plastic template to use as a stencil for the tuiles. The top of an ice-cream container lid works well. Cut out four rectangular holes (leave gaps in between), approx. 2 x 6cm, and discard the pieces you have removed.

piping set

LARDER

REDUCTIONS & PEARLS

There are a whole host of simple modern techniques that can lift a plate of food from plain to trendy. These include the use of powders, gels, reductions and pearls. Both balsamic and soy reductions give you those flamboyant swirling black lines when applied from a squeezy bottle moments before the dish is presented. Pearls are tiny mouth-explosion bombs that add intrigue, great flavour and style and are applied with a medical syringe.

SOY REDUCTION

The soy reduction heightens savoury flavours.

Ingredients
250ml dark soy sauce
2 tbsp sugar
2 tsp arrowroot powder
1 tbsp cold water

MAKES APPROX. 125ML

• Heat the soy sauce and the sugar together in a small heavy-based pan over a moderate heat.

• Bring to the boil then turn down the heat and simmer gently until reduced by half.

• Thoroughly mix the arrowroot powder with the cold water in a cup.

• Stir the arrowroot into the simmering soy reduction, then cook for a further half-minute to thicken.

• Remove from the heat. Allow to cool and apply from a squeezy bottle just before a dish is served. It will keep for up to 3 months.

BALSAMIC REDUCTION

The balsamic vinegar will add sweetness and acidity.

Ingredients
250ml balsamic vinegar

MAKES APPROX. 125ML

• Place the balsamic vinegar in a small heavy-based pan over a moderate heat.

• Bring to the boil then turn down the heat and simmer gently until reduced by half. It should become a nice shiny glaze.

• Remove from the heat at once and allow to cool.

• When cool, transfer to a plastic squeezy bottle and store at room temperature.

• The balsamic reduction will keep for many months. If it gets too thick you can reheat it and add a tablespoon of water.

BALSAMIC PEARLS

An explosion of flavour with the appearance of caviar.

Ingredients

600ml sunflower oil
(can be reused)

100ml balsamic vinegar

½ tsp agar-agar

Equipment

small medical syringe

• Place the oil in an open plastic jug or container and put in the freezer for 3 hours.

• Put the vinegar in a small pan, whisk in the agar-agar. Allow to soak for 2 minutes, then place over a low heat and bring to the boil. Allow to cool for 3 minutes.

• Bring the oil out of the freezer. Fill the syringe with warm vinegar and gently squeeze droplets into the cold oil. They will instantly form into perfectly round little black pearls.

• Store the pearls in oil and lift out with a slotted spoon when required.

MANGO PEARLS

Dots of brightly coloured intense tropical fruit.

Ingredients

600ml sunflower oil
(can be reused)

100ml mango purée

½ tsp agar-agar

Equipment

small medical syringe

• Follow the method exactly as for Balsamic Pearls, using mango purée instead of balsamic vinegar.

ROMESCO SAUCE

There was a time in the City of London when exotic-sounding sauces (unless, of course, they were classic French) were definitely something to be wary of – and a young chef would be going out on a limb suggesting such a thing. Today we now all crave something exotic or unusual. Romesco sauce is a lovely wholesome Mediterranean salsa with centuries of tradition. It is a marvellous larder staple that can be used straight from the fridge to enhance any fish, vegetable or meat dish that seems a little plain or even old-fashioned.

MAKES APPROX. 250ML

Ingredients

1 red pepper

2 tomatoes

120ml olive oil

1 garlic clove

1 tbsp tomato purée

75g blanched almonds, roasted

1 tsp sweet paprika

1 tsp smoked paprika

2 tbsp red wine vinegar

salt and black pepper

Equipment

pestle and mortar

• Put the red pepper and tomatoes with a little of the olive oil into a small roasting tin and cook in a preheated oven at 180°C/gas mark 6 for 12 minutes.

• Using a small knife, peel off the skins, deseed and roughly chop.

• Place the peppers, tomatoes and cooking juices into a mortar.

• Add the garlic, tomato purée, roasted almonds and paprikas. Use the pestle to pound to a textured paste.

• Add the rest of the olive oil and the red wine vinegar. Season to taste with the salt and pepper.

• Transfer to an airtight glass jar and store in the fridge for up to 1 month.

THE CLINK

The City of London is very forward thinking when it comes to embracing new ideas and has welcomed The Clink as a City caterer.

The Clink is a charity set up to create opportunities for inmates of Her Majesty's prisons and other disadvantaged Londoners. Produce is grown in prison market gardens, food production is at HMP Downview and young homeless people from Centrepoint are trained to NVQ Hospitality standards to provide good service. It is a social enterprise project among the very best.

The Clink kindly provided a recipe contribution for this book but unfortunately on this occasion it could not be fitted in. Nonetheless I endorse their work and hope to find another opportunity to cook with their team.

WHIPPED ANCHOVY BUTTER

Gentlemen's Relish is a well-known patented product that can easily be associated with City Livery Companies or private members' clubs. But the concept of a strongly flavoured anchovy butter is useful to every cook in every kitchen – this, for me, is a larder essential. Anchovy butter can be used to enhance all sorts of dishes from grilled lamb or fish to scrambled eggs, or just spread on scones or toast for high tea.

- Make sure the butter is at room temperature then, using a balloon or electric hand whisk, beat it in a mixing bowl until smooth and fluffy.
- Finely chop the anchovy fillets, then whisk them into the butter along with the lemon zest, juice and herbs.
- Add the nutmeg. Season to taste with the pepper.
- Serve with toast, or transfer to a storage jar and store in the fridge for up to 4 weeks.

Ingredients

150g unsalted butter, softened

12 canned anchovy fillets in oil, drained

1 lemon, juice and zest

1 tsp finely chopped fresh thyme

1 tsp finely chopped fresh chives

freshly grated nutmeg

black pepper

To serve

toast

DINING WITH THE JUDGES AT THE OLD BAILEY

In the 18th and 19th centuries, dining was a key part of the court sessions at the Old Bailey and it was customary for the City Sheriff and Aldermen to host two dinners each day in order that judges and court officials might attend either sitting. It was not uncommon, however, for the more indulgent to attend both. Wine also flowed freely. There is a record dated 1807 stating that 145 dozen bottles of wine were consumed over 19 days of court sessions. Often the judges would pass sentence having been disturbed from their feasting with 'their wigs well oiled'.

I am sure everyone will be relieved to learn that, although the Sheriffs and Judges still dine together at the Old Bailey, alcohol is now not served.

SPRINKLES & POWDERS

This is an odd title to find in a recipe book, but powders are another great weapon to have in your larder to enhance flavour and presentation. A little sprinkle here, a delicate shading there or a splash of colour – powders can add another dimension to a dish. Some powders can just be bought off the shelf, such as sweet or hot paprika, cinnamon or dried basil, but below are some ideas and techniques to get you underway creating your own repertoire. You will need a dehydrator or an oven that can be left on very low overnight, such as the warming oven on an Aga, and a food processor or liquidizer.

MUSHROOM POWDER

For intense umami flavour.

Ingredients

400g mushroom peelings or offcuts (it is a waste to use whole mushrooms, although of course, you can)

salt and ground white pepper

• Place the mushroom offcuts on a baking tray in a very low oven (or dehydrator) overnight.

• Allow the offcuts to dry out and shrivel.

• Season to taste with salt and pepper.

• Blitz in a food processor until you have a fine powder.

• Transfer to an airtight storage jar.

BUTTERNUT SQUASH WITH HAZELNUTS

For sweetness, nuttiness and crunch.

Ingredients

400g butternut squash, peeled, cored and thinly sliced

100g hazelnuts

salt and black pepper

• Lay the butternut squash slices on a tin and into a dehydrator or very low oven overnight.

• Roast the hazelnuts in a preheated oven at 180°C/gas mark 6 for 10 minutes.

• Transfer the butternut squash and the hazelnuts to a food processor and season to taste with salt and pepper.

• Blitz to a fine powder.

• Transfer to an airtight storage jar.

LEEK ASH

For a charcoal vegetable flavour.

Ingredients

400g leeks, cut lengthways into
long ribbons

- Place the leeks in a dry baking tin and cook in a preheated oven at 220°C/gas mark 9 for 20 minutes.

- Transfer the blackened leeks to a food processor and blitz to a coarse powder.

- Transfer to an airtight storage jar.

RASPBERRY, MANGO OR KIWI POWDERS

For vibrant colour and extra taste.

Ingredients
Fruits of your choice, sliced

- Lay the prepared fruits out on a baking tray.

- Thoroughly dry them out in a very low oven or a dehydrator.

- Blitz to a fine powder using a food processor.

- Transfer to an airtight container... I am sure you are getting the idea.

VEGETABLE, FRUIT & SAVOURY GELS

Agar-agar is made from seaweed and is an amazing vegetarian substitute for gelatine to use as a setting agent. It is not the same as gelatine, though; it makes a firmer gel and does not melt in the mouth, so it is not ideal in traditional fruit jellies or mousses. It has, however, opened up a whole new spectrum of culinary possibilities and is well worth experimenting with.

HERB & FLORA JELLY MAT

The jelly mat is an amazing visual base to use for stylish starters and cold plates. This recipe can be adapted for desserts by using melon juice in place of cucumber.

Ingredients

2 cucumbers, peeled and roughly chopped

approx. 200ml water

1 ½ tsp agar-agar

1 tsp salt

1 punnet of micro herbs

edible pansies

Equipment

muslin, for fine straining

• Put the chopped cucumbers in a liquidizer along with the water.

• Strain through a sieve lined with a piece of muslin over a bowl. Squeeze out all remaining cucumber juice, discarding the pulp.

• Measure the juice and add more water if necessary to make up to 500ml. Add the salt.

• Put the liquid in a small pan and, using an electric hand whisk, beat the agar-agar in. Leave to soak for a couple of minutes.

• Place the pan over a low heat, slowly bring to the boil and simmer for 2–3 minutes.

• Pour a thin layer onto a very flat tray. Dot on the micro herbs and pansy petals immediately.

• Leave to set. The jelly mat can then be cut and handled.

FRUIT GEL

Fruit gels can be used for sweet or savoury dishes – and they don't melt on a hot plate. Rhubarb, redcurrant, cranberry or blackberry all work really well.

Ingredients
250ml fruit purée
250g caster sugar
250ml water
I tsp agar-agar

- Begin by making or buying a good-quality whole fruit unsweetened purée, not juice.

- Place the sugar and water in a small pan over a low heat and stir until the sugar is fully dissolved.

- Transfer to a measuring jug. Make sure you have 250ml of sugar syrup and allow to cool.

- Put the sugar syrup and fruit purée back in the pan and, using an electric hand whisk, beat in the agar-agar.

- Allow to stand for a couple of minutes then place over a low heat. Bring to the boil and allow to simmer for 2–3 minutes.

- Pour the mixture into a shallow tin and chill to set.

- Turn the set jelly out onto a chopping board and cut into cubes.

- Transfer to a liquidizer and blitz to make the gel. You may want to add a little water at this stage to achieve the desired consistency.

- The gel can now be used in a piping bag, squeezy bottle or just by the spoonful.

SAVOURY GEL

Savoury gels are made just as above but without the sugar and are seasoned with salt, pepper or spices. A huge variety of vegetable gels are possible from your own vegetable purées – spinach, pumpkin and red pepper will give you a perfect set of traffic lights!

HARVY SCARVY NORFOLK RELISH

The resource of having a few secret ingredients in your larder cannot be underestimated. It is how to take your cooking from average to something very special. This unusual summer relish is very fresh, tangy and a great accompaniments for pâtés, cheeses or salads. Sometimes it is just the name that can make something appealing. We found a version of Harvy Scarvy in a very old recipe collection from the 1930s and simply couldn't resist.

MAKES APPROX. 500ml

Ingredients

60ml red wine vinegar

60ml olive oil

3 celery sticks, finely diced

2 firm red apples, cored but peel left on, finely diced

1 small red onion, finely diced

120g redcurrants, pulled off the stalk

salt and black pepper

• Combine all the ingredients together in a mixing bowl and season to taste.

• Leave the flavours to infuse for a minimum of 3 hours.

• Transfer to an airtight jar and serve when you wish.

• Store in the fridge for up to 4 weeks.

An Elizabethan Cook's Grace used at the Cooks' Company Banquets

For bread and salt, for grapes and malt
For flesh and fish and every dish
Mutton and beefe and meaty cheefe
For cowheals, chitterlings, tripes and sowse
And other meats that's in the house.
For fritters, pancakes and for fries
For venison, pastries and mince pies
Sheepshead, garlic, brawne and mustard
Wafers, cakes, tart and custard.

MAYONNAISE

The next larder essential is good old-fashioned mayonnaise. It is both satisfying to make and a completely different product from even the best-quality manufactured mayonnaise. Mayonnaise is constantly used in an active kitchen for everything from sandwich fillings, to dressings, salads and savoury mousses or just as a side.

MAKES APPROX. 400ml

- Using an electric hand whisk (or balloon whisk if you wish), beat the egg yolks, mustards and vinegar together in a medium-sized bowl.

- Season to taste with salt and plenty of pepper.

- Whisking continuously, start to slowly add the oil, just a few drops at first and then a tablespoonful at a time.

- It will take approximately 5 minutes of whisking before all the oil is incorporated and the base mayonnaise is complete.

- Finally, stir in any additions.

- Cover the bowl with clingfilm and transfer to the fridge. The mayonnaise will keep well in the fridge for up to 10 days.

Ingredients

2 large egg yolks (save the whites for meringue)

2 tsp Dijon mustard

1 tbsp wholegrain mustard

1 tbsp cider vinegar

salt and black pepper

300ml sunflower oil

Optional additions

Lemon mayonnaise – add the juice and zest of 2 lemons.

Tarragon mayonnaise – add 1 heaped tablespoon of finely chopped fresh tarragon leaves and a little lemon juice.

Thousand island dressing – add 1 tablespoon of tomato purée and a few drops of Tabasco sauce.

Tartar sauce – add chopped gherkins, capers and lemon juice.

MARMALADES & FERMENTS

The culinary arts of bottling, pickling, preserving and fermenting are as old as civilization itself. Before cans, freezers and vacuum packs were invented, these methods were the only ways of keeping fruits and vegetables through the winter months. Fermenting is now very much in fashion and there are plenty of books on the subject. But here is a contrasting marmalade and a ferment of vegetables to get you started. The first step for all preserving is to properly sterilize the jars. Thoroughly wash, then drain the jars upside down until dry. Place the jars and lids on a baking tray and put them into the oven at 180°C/gas mark 6 for 20 minutes. Lift out the jars and allow to cool before using them.

FENNEL & KUMQUAT MARMALADE

A delicious savoury marmalade that complements poultry, game, pork or cooked cheese dishes.

MAKES 2 X 250ml JARS

Ingredients
25ml rapeseed oil
2 small red onions, cut into strips
2 fennel bulbs, cored and cut crossways into strips
120g kumquats, sliced
1 lime, juice and zest
2 tbsp soft brown sugar
salt and black pepper

• Heat the oil in a medium heavy-based pan over a low heat.

• Gently fry the onion and allow to caramelize, but do not allow to brown.

• Add the fennel, kumquat and lime. Continue to cook gently for 30 minutes, stirring occasionally.

• Once the fennel has fully softened add the sugar, season to taste with salt and pepper and turn up the heat.

• Boil rapidly until the juice evaporates and the mixture is the consistency of jam. Remove from the heat and transfer to the jars.

• Seal and store until ready to use.

FERMENTED BROCCOLI WITH CARROT, RADISH & SPRING ONION

This is a great Korean-style ferment that can lift any meal.
It can be served as a side, salad or relish.

MAKES 2 X 250ml JARS

Ingredients

2 garlic cloves, roughly chopped

1 tsp grated root ginger

1 tsp finely diced fresh red chilli

20g rock salt (2% of the vegetable weight)

50g golden caster sugar

20ml white wine vinegar

500g broccoli, cut into long thin strips, including the stalks

250g carrots, peeled and cut into matchsticks

1 bunch radishes, cut into small wedges

6 spring onions, shredded

Equipment

pestle and mortar

• Crush the garlic, ginger, chilli and salt using a pestle and mortar, then add the sugar and vinegar to form a paste.

• Place the prepared vegetables in a large mixing bowl. Add the paste and mix them together.

• Leave to marinate for 30 minutes; some of the vegetable juices will be released.

• Now pack the vegetables into sterilized jars, pressing them in with a wooden spoon.

• Top up with a little water to fill the jars. Seal and leave in a cool place to ferment for a minimum of 7 days.

• The flavours will continue to develop the longer the ferment is stored. Once a jar is opened it should be kept in the fridge and used within 2 weeks.

'I do not like broccoli. And I haven't liked it since I was a little kid and my mother made me eat it. And I'm President of the United States and I'm not going to eat any more broccoli.'
George H.W. Bush

STARTERS

KITCHEN GARDEN ENSEMBLE

This is a pretty starter that captures the essence and charm of a vegetable garden in the height of the English summer. Asparagus, baby leeks, courgettes and nasturtiums are complemented by feta cheese, quail egg and Parmesan crisp. It is not essential to grow all the ingredients yourself, but I hope you can enter the garden in spirit while preparing the dish.

SERVES 6

Ingredients

30g Parmesan, finely grated

15 asparagus spears, trimmed

1 baby leek

2 courgettes (approx. 250g)

6 quail eggs

Herb & Flora Jelly Mat
(see page 46)

chives, finely chopped

Basic Dressing (see page 160)

60g feta cheese, cut into
small cubes

nigella seeds (black onion
seeds)

To garnish

6 nasturtium flowers

18 small nasturtium leaves

Equipment

5cm pastry cutter

wide-mouth peeler

• Begin by making the Parmesan crisps.

• Oil a baking tray and then line with baking paper. Place the 5cm pastry cutter on the tray and use it as a stencil. Fill the cutter with approximately one-sixth of the grated Parmesan.

• Lift the cutter off and repeat to make six neat piles spaced apart.

• Place the cheese in a preheated oven at 180°C/gas mark 6 for 5 minutes. The cheese will melt and lightly golden. Set aside to cool.

• Blanch the asparagus in boiling lightly salted water for 3 minutes. Lift out and transfer to a bowl of iced water.

• Cut the leek into six long strips, blanch for 2 minutes, then transfer to the iced water to chill.

• Cut the courgettes into long strips using the wide-mouth peeler. Blanch and then chill.

• Cook the quail eggs in the boiling water for exactly 90 seconds, then plunge into the iced water. Leave the eggs for several minutes, then carefully peel off the shell.

• Remove the asparagus and leek from the water and split the asparagus spears lengthways. Tie small bundles of the split spears together with the strips of baby leek.

• To assemble the dish, cut the Herb & Flora Jelly Mat into six 10 x 4cm rectangles and lay them on individual plates.

• Cut the quail eggs in half. Toss the courgette and chives in a little Basic Dressing.

• Arrange the courgette ribbons, feta and nigella seeds on one end of the herb jelly, and the asparagus, quail egg and Parmesan crisp on the other.

• Garnish with the nasturtium flowers and leaves.

'Creativity is contagious, pass it on.'
Albert Einstein

MELON & STRAWBERRY SOUP

Recipe contributed by Sir Donald H. Brydon, former Chairman of the London Stock Exchange

One of the great institutions synonymous with the City of London is the Stock Exchange. Trading first began on a casual basis in London's backstreet coffee houses. The Royal Exchange was founded in 1566 to formalize trading and is one of the oldest financial institutions in the world. Where in the hectic world of trading stocks and shares the Chairman of the Stock Exchange found the time to enjoy a chilled and refreshing soup I don't know, but Sir Donald assures me that on a hot summer's afternoon this starter is hard to beat. Now there's an inside tip for your broker!

SERVES 6

Ingredients

**2 cantaloupe
(or Charentais) melons**

3 tbsp runny honey

2 lemons, juice and zest

**175ml unsweetened
apple juice**

125g fresh strawberries

250g carton of lemon sorbet

• Remove the skin and any unripe edges from the melons and remove all the seeds. Chop the melon into small pieces.

• Blitz the melon, honey and lemon juice together in a food processor. Add the apple juice. Transfer to the fridge to chill and also chill your serving bowls.

• Cut the strawberries into thin slices.

• Serve the soup in individual bowls with a scoop of sorbet, sliced strawberries and the lemon zest.

• Now all you need is a glass of ice-cold Provençal rosé to enjoy alongside.

WATERCRESS & ALMOND SOUP

This lovely pale green soup combines the fresh peppery flavour of watercress with the nutty body of ground almonds. Susie Robinson first produced this soup when we started Party Ingredients Private Catering together back in 1975 – and I still get regular requests for both the dish and the recipe. I serve the soup with some handmade sesame grissini.

SERVES 6

• Melt the butter in a large heavy-based pan over a moderate heat. Add the potatoes, one bunch of the watercress, lemon zest and almonds. Toss together for about 1 minute.

• Add the stock and milk. Bring to the boil and simmer for 20 minutes. When the potatoes are cooked, transfer the mixture to a food processor and blitz until smooth. Add salt and pepper to taste.

• The soup can now be stored in the fridge and reheated when needed.

• Just before serving, finely chop the remaining bunch of watercress and stir it through the soup to finish, saving a sprig to garnish.

Ingredients

15g butter

225g potatoes, diced

2 bunches watercress

1 lemon, zest

100g ground almonds

600ml chicken stock

600ml milk

salt and black pepper

THE ADVANTAGE OF FAMILY PLANNING

It is not that I wanted to create a food dynasty nor was there any genetic modification involved. But, conveniently, my youngest son Gregory (who does not like photographs and is therefore not shown) is a farmer in Sussex, producing livestock, some vegetables and, of course, grapes in the vineyards. Oliver, our middle son, is the Gladwin restaurant group's Executive Chef and Richard, the eldest, manages the restaurants where the livestock, vegetables and wine are, of course, sold.

I will permit myself a small advert here. The restaurants are The Shed in Notting Hill; Rabbit in King's Road, Chelsea; Nutbourne in Battersea and, soon to come, Sussex in Soho. Their own story is told in *The Shed: The Cookbook*.

LAMB SHANK PITHIVIER WITH ZA'ATAR YOGHURT

Pithivier pies can be sweet or savoury. They are comprised of two layers of puff pastry with a ball, rather than a layer, of filling in between. We have made rabbit, partridge and braised lamb pithiviers as unusual first courses for fine City dinners. They are particularly good as a prelude to a fish main course. This recipe gives a method for cooking lamb shank from scratch, but the dish works well using up leftover cooked meats.

SERVES 6

• Heat the oil in an ovenproof casserole dish over a moderate heat and brown the lamb shank all over. Lift out the lamb and set aside.

• Place the onion in the pan and cook until lightly browned. Add the garlic, rosemary, tomato purée, lamb stock and red wine.

• Return the shank to the dish and bring to a simmer. Cover the casserole with a lid and place in a preheated oven at 180°C/gas mark 6 for 2–2½ hours. The meat should be very tender and fall off the bone.

• Remove the shank from the casserole dish and allow to cool. Return the dish to the heat and reduce the liquid down to approximately 60ml.

• Pull the flesh of the lamb off the bone and shred into small pieces. Place half the lamb in a food processor and pulse it to a rough mince. Combine all the lamb and reduced juices, season to taste.

• Unroll the pastry onto a floured work surface and cut out six discs using the 8cm cutter and six discs using the 9cm cutter.

• Divide the lamb mixture into six balls and place in the centre of the 8cm discs. Brush the rim with beaten egg and then cover the lamb with the 9cm pastry discs. Push down around the filling, then pinch the two layers of pastry together to seal the pie.

• Score the pastry from the centre outwards. Brush with beaten egg and place on an oiled and lined baking sheet, ready to bake.

• Sauté the leeks with a little oil in a pan over a moderate heat until tender (8–10 minutes). Season to taste with salt and pepper and keep warm.

• Bake the pithiviers in the preheated oven at 190°C/gas mark 7 for 18–20 minutes until golden brown.

• Mix the yoghurt, za'atar and lemon zest together and season with salt and pepper.

• Serve on a bed of fried leeks with za'atar yoghurt mixture, radishes and herb oil to complete the dish.

Ingredients

2 tbsp olive oil, plus extra for oiling and frying

500g lamb shank (or 240g leftover cooked lamb)

1 onion, roughly chopped

1 garlic clove

3 rosemary sprigs

1 tbsp tomato purée

100ml lamb stock

100ml red wine

2 x 320g sheets ready-roll puff pastry

1 egg, beaten

350g leeks, trimmed and shredded

salt and black pepper

To finish

150ml Greek thick-set yoghurt

3 tsp za'atar

zest of ½ lemon

1 bunch radishes, stemmed and halved

green herb oil, for drizzling

Equipment

8cm and 9cm pastry cutters

WOOD PIGEON SALTIMBOCCA

My son, Oliver, and I developed this recipe for 'The Shed' cookbook and it has been a favourite for both City dining and in the Gladwin restaurants ever since. Saltimbocca is an ancient Italian dish, traditionally using veal infused with sage and wrapped in prosciutto. Here we are substituting wood pigeon for the veal and finishing the dish with red grapes and pan juices.

SERVES 6

Ingredients

6 wood pigeon breasts, or 12 if you want more

6 sage leaves

6 thin slices of lemon

26 long slices of Parma ham

60g unsalted butter

25ml red wine

2 tsp balsamic vinegar

2 tsp honey

2 tsp French mustard

120g red grapes, halved and seeded

salt and black pepper

To serve

mixed salad leaves

• Place the pigeon breasts on a chopping board and carefully cut a slot across the middle of each one without cutting into two.

• Put a sage leaf and a slice of lemon inside each one. Wrap a slice of ham around to form a parcel. Season to taste with salt and pepper.

• Heat a heavy-based frying pan over a moderate heat and melt the butter.

• Fry the pigeon breasts for 2–3 minutes on each side. Remove from the pan and keep warm.

• Return the frying pan to a high heat and quickly add the red wine, balsamic, honey and mustard. Stir rapidly, let it sizzle and deglaze the pan, then toss in the grapes.

• Carve the pigeon breasts into three and serve on a bed of salad leaves. Spoon over the glaze with the grapes and serve immediately.

MICHAELMAS GOOSE

There is an ancient tradition of eating goose on the feast of St Michael, known as Michaelmas, on 29 September. Sometimes the day was known as 'goose day' and goose fairs were held.

Michaelmas is the start of autumn, harvest is over and new farm tenancies begin.

There is a saying that goes: 'Eat a goose on Michaelmas Day; want not for money all the year.' Geese are also grass-reared in the summer months and therefore less fatty than a Christmas goose that has been fed on wheat.

Alas, there is no goose recipe in this book, but you can substitute a goose with a tiny wood pigeon.

LONDON GIN-CURED TROUT WITH TONIC & LIME GEL

In the 18th century there were distilleries and gin shops throughout the City. The craze died out nearly 200 years ago, but the popularity of boutique gins has now resurged. The Square Mile even has its own micro distillery – the City of London Distillery situated in Bride Lane. This stylish modern starter presents gin and tonic with a difference – and whether you are a fan of the drink or not, it is a great way to cure and present rainbow trout.

SERVES 6–8

• Check the trout fillets are fully boned by running your finger along the flesh. Use a pair of tweezers to pin bone any that remain. Place the fillets as an even layer in a shallow dish.

• Blitz the juniper berries and star anise in a food processor into a fine powder. Mix the spices with the sugar, salt, gin and dill.

• Spread the mixture evenly over the fish, cover with clingfilm and leave to cure in the fridge for 12 hours.

• Prepare the tonic and lime gel using Indian tonic water and lime juice in place of water (see page 47, for gels), saving the lime zest for garnish.

• Split the cucumber lengthways, remove the seeds and slice into half moons. Dress with a little vinegar, sugar and salt. Leave for 20 minutes.

• Drain the juice off the cucumber, add the beetroot juice and pour over the shallots to lightly pickle.

• Wash the cure off the trout fillets under cold water. Carve into neat thin slices (approximately 3mm).

• Arrange the sliced trout on individual plates with the pickled cucumber and shallots.

• Pipe the tonic gel onto the plate and finish with caviar or roe and lime zest, and a sprinkle of pepper.

Ingredients

4 rainbow trout fillets

For the cure

1 tbsp juniper berries

2 tsp star anise

80g sugar

80g salt

2 tbsp London Dry Gin

1 bunch of dill, roughly chopped

For the gel

250ml Indian tonic water

2 limes, juice and zest, reserving the zest for garnish

1 tsp agar-agar

To finish

1 cucumber

1 tsp white wine vinegar

1 tsp caster sugar

1 tbsp beetroot juice, from a carton is fine

2 shallots, finely sliced

20g keta caviar or lumpfish roe

salt and black pepper

Equipment

tweezers

piping set

MACKEREL & SEABASS TERRINE

Fish terrines are sometimes considered a little bit old-fashioned, but they can still be a lovely starter. The core principles must be to season well, preserve texture by avoiding pulping the fish and beautiful presentation – look at the lovely snapdragons we have used to garnish the dish, straight from the garden.

SERVES 6

Ingredients

2 x seabass fillets (200g)

150ml mayonnaise

100ml double cream

1 lemon, juice and zest

1 tbsp anchovy essence

1 bunch of chives, finely chopped

a few drops of Tabasco

3 tsp powdered gelatine

1 bunch of Swiss chard

oil, for oiling

100g smoked mackerel fillets, flaked

salt and black pepper

To finish

Salsa Verde (see page 164)

edible snapdragon flowers

Equipment

135mm U-shaped terrine tin

• Place the seabass fillets in an ovenproof dish and cover with hot water. Poach in a preheated oven at 180°C/gas mark 6 for 6 minutes until just cooked. Remove from the poaching liquid and allow to cool. Reserve 40ml of the poaching liquor and discard the rest.

• Once cool, remove and discard the skin of the seabass. Flake the fish into a mixing bowl, add the mayonnaise, double cream, lemon zest, anchovy essence, chives and a few drops of Tabasco. Mix together and season to taste.

• Put the reserved fish liquor into a small pan and stir in the gelatine. Leave to swell for 3–4 minutes, then place over a low heat to gently dissolve.

• Oil and line the terrine tin with a generous double layer of clingfilm. Blanch the Swiss chard in boiling salted water for a few moments, then refresh under cold water and dry on a tea towel.

• Remove stems from the chard and line the tin with leaves. Leave a flap hanging over the edge to fold over once filled.

• Add the dissolved gelatine to the fish mixture and stir in well. Gently mix in the mackerel flakes without breaking them up. Pour a third of the mixture into the tin, add a few more chard leaves, pour the next third and layer again. Fold over the edge flaps to encase the whole terrine.

• Transfer to the fridge and allow to set for 3–4 hours.

• Slice the terrine with a very sharp knife. Finish with the Salsa Verde and the edible flowers.

REGIMENTAL FIRE

The Honourable Artillery Company (HAC) is one of the oldest army corps in the world.

'Regimental Fire' is the toast given by members to fellow members. It takes the form of a nine-fold shout of the word 'zay' together with some obscure arm movements. Apparently it originates from when all good chaps would be given three cheers (or in this case 'zays'), and particularly good chaps (such as members of the HAC) would be given three times three cheers, hence nine. As a non-member guest, you will be toasted with 'silent fire' – still lots of arm movements but only a single 'zay' on the ninth thrust.

BEETROOT RAVIOLI WITH BROAD BEANS & EDAMAME PESTO

Pasta-making is said to be very therapeutic and is a culinary skill well worth developing. If you don't already have one, you will need to invest in a small hand-operated pasta-making machine. These ravioli combine the natural sweetness of beetroot with ricotta and, if the pasta is thin enough, the beetroot colour attractively shines through. We are serving them with a scattering of double-podded broad beans and an edamame bean pesto.

SERVES 6

- Put the flour and salt into a large mixing bowl, make a well in the middle and pour in the eggs and oil. Use your fingertips to work the flour into the eggs from round the edge of the well until it is all combined.

- Sprinkle semolina onto a work surface and turn the pasta dough onto it. Knead energetically for 4 minutes, until the dough is smooth and elastic. Divide the dough into three lumps the size of an orange, wrap tightly in clingfilm and refrigerate for 1 hour.

- Meanwhile, prepare the filling by combining the grated beetroot with the ricotta, thyme and seasoning.

- Take a ball of dough from the fridge, remove the clingfilm, dust with semolina and roll out a little with a rolling pin, ready to feed into the pasta machine.

- Feed the dough through on the widest setting, then fold all the sides inwards, turn by 90° and feed it through again. Repeat this process several times. This makes the dough more pliable and creates a mesh from the gluten that will prevent the pasta from splitting. Keep dusting with a little extra semolina to prevent the dough from becoming sticky.

- Adjust the rollers on the pasta machine to the next setting and roll the dough through again. Continue to roll the dough through the machine, decreasing the thickness by one setting each time until it is 2mm thick.

- Cover the rolled pasta with a damp tea towel until ready to make the ravioli.

- Dust a work surface with semolina flour and place the rolled pasta on it. Use the fluted cutter to cut out a few discs at a time. Place a small spoonful of the beetroot mixture on a disc and a second disc on top. Pinch the edges to make a seal.

- Store the ravioli on a baking tray dusted with semolina in a single layer and keep in the fridge until ready to cook.

- Prepare the edamame pesto by blending all the ingredients together in a food processor to form a paste.

- Cook the ravioli in a large pan of lightly salted water for 3 minutes. Lift out of the water with a slotted spoon, sprinkle with a little extra oil and serve immediately with the edamame pesto, a scattering of broad beans and a small bouquet of purple cress.

Ingredients

400g of 00 grade flour

½ tsp salt

4 large eggs, lightly beaten

1 tbsp rapeseed oil

a little semolina flour, for dusting

For the filling

3 large beetroot, roasted then finely grated

200g ricotta

3 thyme sprigs, leaves only, finely chopped

salt and black pepper

For the pesto

250g edamame beans

1 bunch of fresh basil

3 tbsp lemon juice

2 tbsp water

1 garlic clove

100ml olive oil

To finish

a little extra olive oil

200g double-podded broad beans, blanched

purple cress

Equipment

hand-operated pasta-maker

6cm fluted cutter

KING SCALLOPS & SAMPHIRE SEAFOOD BISQUE

Recipe contributed by Fabrice Lasnon, Executive Chef of The Savoy, London

The Savoy Hotel was the first luxury hotel in London and Auguste Escoffier its first head chef. Without hesitation their Executive Chef Fabrice Lasnon agreed to contribute to this book – but the Savoy 'recipes' are chef specification sheets instructing sections within their kitchens to produce different elements of a dish. Their delicious seafood bisque began with instructions to prepare 10,000g of lobster and 10,000g of crab – so those of you making this at home might have been a little put off before you started! So forgive me, Fabrice Lasnon, we have taken your inspiration and put together our own version, which we hope does justice to the Savoy's tremendous heritage.

SERVES 6

Ingredients

120g samphire

6 large king scallops

pinch of saffron

salt and black pepper

a few drops of Tabasco

a little oil, for coating

For the bisque

3 tbsp oil

1 onion, diced

1 garlic clove, sliced

3 celery sticks, diced

3 carrots, diced

1 leek, cleaned and chopped

3 sprigs of thyme, leaves only

1 bay leaf

240g prawns, with shells on

240g seafood, such as crab, mussel meat or squid

240g canned tomatoes

120g jar of pimentos

200ml white wine

400ml fish stock

2 lemons, juice and zest, reserving the zest for garnish

50ml brandy

100ml double cream

Equipment

stick blender (optional)

ribbed griddle pan

• Begin by making the seafood bisque. Heat the oil in a large heavy-based pan over a medium heat. Sweat the onion, garlic, celery, carrot, leek, thyme and bay until soft but not brown.

• Add the prawns and seafood. Cook for 5 minutes. Stir in the tomatoes, pimentos, wine, stock and lemon juice, saving the lemon zest for garnish. Season to taste. Turn down the heat and simmer for 45 minutes.

• Scoop out any hard shells, such as mussel or oyster, but leave the prawn shells. Use a stick blender or food processor to purée all the ingredients.

• Pass the mixture first through a colander then a sieve into a clean pan ready to reheat before serving.

• Prepare the samphire by first soaking it in cold water for 30 minutes. Drain and rinse well. Blanch in unsalted boiling water for 3 minutes.

• Make sure the king scallops are carefully trimmed – take off the side muscle but leave the coral. Lightly coat the scallops with oil, season to taste with salt and pepper, and sprinkle with a very few strands of saffron and a little Tabasco.

• Reheat the bisque and stir in the brandy and cream.

• Heat the ribbed griddle pan to very hot. Sear the scallops on all sides with no more than 3 minutes' cooking. They should be scorched on the outside but still pearly in the middle.

• Serve immediately on a bed of samphire, with the bisque poured around. Finish with the lemon zest.

'A woman should never be seen eating or drinking, unless it be lobster salad and Champagne, the only true feminine and becoming viands.'

Lord Byron

DUCK LIVER PARFAIT
WITH SPICED APPLE

There is a certain institution in the City that prides itself in its gourmet reputation and serves very fine wines to match. One of its prerequisites is that our resident chef should produce terrines, pâtés or parfaits on a very regular basis. The differences between the three are a little blurred – but generally the terrines are chunkier, the pâtés smoother but meatier and the parfaits lighter with the addition of cream or egg white. All three complement top-quality oak-aged white Burgundy very well and that is the important factor.

SERVES 6

- Oil and line the terrine tin with a double layer of clingfilm.

- Soften 100g of the butter in a microwave. Liberally brush all over the lined tin, leave to set in the fridge and then repeat to make a thick layer.

- Trim any membrane and sinew from the duck livers and soak in milk for half an hour. Drain and discard the milk.

- Gently heat the remaining butter in a heavy-based pan over a low heat. Fry the onion, garlic and duck livers for approximately 5 minutes until the livers are cooked through.

- Transfer the mixture to a food processor and blitz until completely smooth. Add the cognac, Madeira and cream. Blitz again.

- Place 2 tablespoons of cold water and the gelatine in a small pan. Stir together and allow the gelatine to swell for 4 minutes.

- Gently heat the pan without boiling until the powder is completely dissolved. Stir the gelatine into the liver mixture and season well. Pour into the butter-lined tin. Leave to set overnight.

- Chop the pistachios very finely and lay them on a work surface.

- Lift the parfait out of the tin and remove the clingfilm. Using the blowtorch, gently melt the outer layer of butter and then roll the parfait in the chopped pistachios. Return to the fridge to re-set the butter before serving.

- Make the apple compote by cooking the chopped apple, sugar and spice in a small pan over a low heat until softened.

- Place a thin-bladed sharp knife in a jug of hot water, then use it to slice the parfait.

- Serve the parfait with the apple compote, sprinkled with a few pink peppercorns and herbs to garnish. You could also add a side of crunchy sourdough toast.

Ingredients

150g unsalted butter

200g duck livers

100ml milk

1 onion, finely diced

1 garlic clove

2 tbsp Cognac or Armagnac

2 tbsp Madeira

2 tbsp powdered gelatine

120ml double cream

60g peeled pistachios

salt and black pepper

For the compote

400g Granny Smith or Bramley apples, peeled, cored and chopped

50g light brown sugar

1 tsp mixed spice

1/2 tsp pink peppercorns

herbs, to garnish

Equipment

135mm U-shaped terrine tin

a cooking blowtorch

'An apple a day keeps the doctor away' is a Welsh proverb. But did you know that medical research has apples down as one of the healthiest things we can eat? Rich in antioxidants, an apple a day helps reduce the risk of cancer, hypertension, diabetes and heart disease.

SALADS
& SIDES

ALLOTMENT SALAD

For me, the word 'allotment' captures our strong will to lovingly grow produce on a special piece of ground alongside like-minded others. The City of London only has one small allotment, plus a few community vegetable-growing sites, but the spirit is definitely there. We all love the idea of growing what we eat. It is also an evocative name for a dish.

SERVES 6

Ingredients

12 asparagus spears

12 baby carrots, trimmed

1 bunch of baby beetroot, trimmed and halved

1 bunch of heritage radishes, trimmed and halved

250g punnet mixed cherry tomatoes, halved

300g sourdough bread, cut into rough croûtes and dried out in the oven

Hazelnut Dressing (see page 160)

6 large hen or duck eggs

1 tbsp vinegar

salt and black pepper

Equipment

long-handled sieve

• Prepare a large pot of simmering, lightly salted water and a separate bowl of iced water.

• Blanch the asparagus for 5 minutes, then lift out of the water with a long-handled sieve and plunge into the ice.

• Repeat with the baby carrots.

• Do the same with the beetroot – although these will take longer to cook. Allow 20 minutes and check them before transferring them to the ice.

• Drain all the cooked vegetables and lay them out with the raw radishes and tomatoes.

• Now build your salads. This is what will make the big difference. If you just toss the vegetables together they will never look quite right. Take the trouble to add each one at a time to achieve a seemingly random arrangement.

• Finish with a scattering of the sourdough croûtes and Hazelnut Dressing.

• Renew the simmering water before poaching the eggs. Add the vinegar to the water to help set the whites.

• Break each egg into a cup then smoothly pour them into the water. Cook for 3 minutes, then gently lift out onto kitchen paper.

• Place the poached eggs straight onto the salad while still hot, add a grind of pepper and serve immediately.

SPITALFIELDS MARKET

The old Spitalfields Market was an integral part of the City for 300 years. It has now relocated to a vast 31-acre site in the East End, but is still managed by the City Corporation. Visiting a fruit and vegetable market always gives me the same feeling of heightened senses and elation given by the Spitalfields Market. It is the combination of smells, the bustle and visual rainbow of colour – fruits, flowers and vegetables all grown somewhere to come to market and fulfil their destiny.

RED QUINOA, BABY SPINACH, ORANGE & FETA SALAD

Quinoa ticks a lot of boxes: it is full of protein, fibre and vitamins; it has a lovely texture; it is gluten-free; and it is incredibly trendy. This simple, flavoursome salad is great as a lunch dish or an interesting side for barbecued meats or fish.

SERVES 6

Ingredients

200g red quinoa

2 tbsp Citrus Dressing (see page 160)

100g baby spinach

3 oranges, peeled and segmented

400g feta cheese, roughly cut into small cubes

1 pomegranate, deseeded, reserving the seeds for garnish

150ml natural yoghurt

sumac and salt

• Cook the quinoa in a pan of boiling lightly salted water for 15 minutes.

• Remove the pan from the heat. Allow the quinoa to rest in the water for 5 minutes, then drain.

• Transfer to a salad bowl, add the Citrus Dressing and toss well to coat the seeds.

• Now carefully mix in the baby spinach leaves, orange segments and feta.

• Season the yoghurt with sumac spice and salt to taste, then drizzle onto the salad.

• Complete the salad with the pomegranate seeds.

CAULIFLOWER & ROMANESCO COUSCOUS

For those of us who don't particularly like couscous, grated cauliflowers are the perfect answer. The result looks like couscous; and it is a perfect side dish for Moroccan lamb or other spiced meats, without being a couscous at all.

SERVES 6–8 (AS A SIDE)

- Using the coarse side of a box grater, grate the cauliflower and Romanesco cauliflower into a large bowl.

- Add the cranberries, olive oil and lemon.

- Toss all the ingredients together and season to taste with salt and pepper.

- Finish with a sprinkling of toasted flaked almonds.

Ingredients

1 cauliflower, cored and broken into florets

1 Romanesco cauliflower, cored and broken into florets

100g dried cranberries

50ml olive oil

2 lemons, juice and grated zest

100g flaked almonds, toasted

salt and black pepper

Grace before Dinner

Grace is a small prayer said before a meal to thank God (not your credit card) for providing it. Some are very religious and others a little more humorous.

Thank you for teaching me gratitude with this delicious bread and meat.

Thank you for teaching me patience while waiting 'til time to eat.

Thank you for teaching me faith, expecting food and never having doubts.

Thank you for teaching me suffering by providing these Brussels sprouts.

STUFFED COURGETTE FLOWERS WITH ROMESCO SAUCE

Courgette flowers are attractive and have a lovely fresh floral taste. They are also now available in good greengrocers for most of the year. This recipe introduces an unusual technique for cooking the baby courgettes without separating them or spoiling the flowers. The flowers can then be filled with all sorts of delicious stuffings ranging from a fish mousse to a cooked lentil mix or, in this case, artichoke hearts with goat's cheese.

SERVES 6

- Prepare a bowl of iced water.

- Fill a small pan almost to the top with water, cover with clingfilm and bring to the boil. Poke six holes in the clingfilm and post the courgettes through the clingfilm so that the baby courgettes (stalks) are immersed in water with the flower heads sitting above.

- Cook for 2–3 minutes, then remove gently from the pan and plunge the hot cooked part into the iced water to refresh. Now you have blanched courgettes and raw flowers.

- Prepare a simple white sauce. Melt the butter in a medium-sized heavy-based pan over a moderate heat, stir in the flour and cook for 1 minute. Stir in the milk a little at a time, add the cheese, season well with salt and pepper and cook until smooth.

- Remove from the heat and stir in the artichokes, sultanas and pine nuts. Allow to cool.

- Carefully fold back the petals of the courgette flowers, place a large spoon of the artichoke mixture inside and rearrange the petals to enclose.

- Place the stuffed courgettes on a serving platter, add the chicory leaves in between and fill these with the Romesco sauce, topped with the chives.

Ingredients

6 courgette flowers, attached to baby courgettes

40g butter

40g plain flour

400ml milk

60g goat's cheese

240g artichoke hearts, diced

60g sultanas

60g pine nuts

1 head red chicory with 6 trimmed leaves

100ml Romesco Sauce (see page 40)

salt and black pepper

chives, finely chopped, to garnish

FORAGER'S WILD MUSHROOMS WITH HAZELNUTS

Foraging in unspoiled woodland and discovering a secret hoard of chanterelles, oyster mushrooms or giant ceps hidden under an oak tree is one of the most exciting and fulfilling experiences a foodie can have. But please be wary: to the inexperienced eye, an innocent looking poisonous toadstool can easily be mistaken for an edible delight. Luckily, there are professional foragers out there who will discover, collect and vet wild mushrooms to be sold. Of course, they monopolize that experience of discovery, but we do get to cook and eat the delicious produce.

SERVES 6

Ingredients

300g assorted wild mushrooms

150g oyster mushrooms

50g cornflour

pinch of ground mace

pinch of cinnamon

80ml rapeseed oil

1 garlic clove, crushed

100g hazelnuts

1 tsp Dijon mustard

1 tsp wholegrain mustard

2 tsp balsamic vinegar

150g wild salad leaves, such as chickweed, dandelion, wood or golden sorrel, or wild rocket

salt and black pepper

• Carefully pick through the wild mushrooms to make sure they are clean. Wash if necessary, but be careful not to saturate them.

• Tear the oyster mushrooms into strips, mix the cornflour with the mace, cinnamon and seasoning, then toss the mushrooms in the flour.

• Heat the oil in a medium-sized heavy-based pan over a moderate heat. Lightly cook the floured oyster mushrooms, then lift them out of the pan onto kitchen paper with a slotted spoon.

• Add the wild mushrooms, garlic and hazelnuts to the pan and fry for 2 minutes. Add the mustards and vinegar and season the dish again.

• Casually arrange the salad leaves on a serving platter. Spoon over the hot wild mushrooms together with all the juices and place the oyster mushrooms in the centre. Serve immediately.

CARROT & ORANGE PURÉE

Heritage carrots can be purple, white, black, yellow or red and are now all the rage. This is how carrots used to grow, and it was only a horticulturist in Holland who decided a uniform orange colour would make the vegetable more commercially appealing. I don't recommend you make a purée from multicoloured heritage carrots unless you want a brown sludge. But I do recommend this orange carrot and orange fruit combination; it is an unusual, tasty side dish that has visual impact.

SERVES 6

- Place a large pan half-filled with water over a moderate heat and bring to the boil.

- Salt the water, add the carrots, cook for 15 minutes, then drain.

- Transfer the carrot to a food processor. Add the orange zest and juice, butter and season well. Blitz to a smooth purée. Transfer to a serving dish.

- Stir in the caraway seeds and either keep warm or reheat when needed.

Ingredients

1 kg carrots, topped, tailed, peeled and cut into chunks

2 oranges, juice and zest

25g butter

1 tbsp caraway seeds, toasted

salt and black pepper

VE DAY BANQUET 1995 – CELEBRATED WITH A BLACKCURRANT LEAF

My own day began at 4.30am in Sussex picking blackcurrant leaves to garnish the Chilled Soufflé of Early Summer Berries. It was the day the world commemorated 50 years since the end of the Second World War and Her Majesty the Queen was the principal guest at a banquet to surpass all others in the City of London's modern history.

Fifty-two Heads of State and representatives from virtually every other country in the world were among the 1,004 guests who were invited for dinner. Five magnificent courses with fine wines to match were served in three different areas of Guildhall. We raised a team of 280 staff, friends, friends of friends, family and volunteers to help serve them. The VE Day banquet was a day and an honour that I will never forget. The full menu is reproduced on page 185.

PARSNIP, SWEET POTATO & AUBERGINE DAUPHINOISE

This is a dauphinoise with a difference. Instead of potatoes we are using parsnips, sweet potatoes (which are not potatoes at all) and aubergines. But they are cooked in the same way as dauphinoise potatoes and make a great side dish. I particularly recommend it for serving with game birds and venison.

SERVES 6

Ingredients

500g aubergines

500g sweet potatoes, peeled

500g parsnips, peeled

600ml double cream

1 garlic clove, crushed

grated nutmeg

1 egg

salt and black pepper

Equipment

mandolin slicer

5cm pastry cutter (optional)

• Halve the aubergines lengthways then slice as thinly as possible.

• Using the mandolin, cut the sweet potatoes and parsnips into 5mm slices. Layer the vegetables in an ovenproof dish.

• Heat the cream in a small heavy-based pan over a low heat with the garlic. Season to taste with nutmeg, salt and plenty of pepper.

• Whisk the egg in a mixing bowl. Add the cream to the egg and whisk together.

• Pour this mixture onto the vegetables, making sure it soaks all the way through.

• Bake in a preheated oven at 180°C/gas mark 6 for 45 minutes.

• The dish is ready to serve. For a more sophisticated presentation the dauphinoise can be cooled, then cut into little castles with a 5cm pastry cutter. Reheat in the oven just before serving.

'Love many things, for therein lies the true strength, and whosoever loves much performs much, and can accomplish much, and what is done in love is done well.'

Vincent van Gogh

COURGETTE & BUTTERNUT SQUASH RIBBONS

We eat with our eyes as well as our mouths and these colourful vegetable ribbons are truly a visual delight. Some foods just can't help being brown and dull-looking, which is when ribbons of butternut squash and courgette come to the rescue.

SERVES 6

- Use the wide-mouth peeler to cut the courgettes and butternut squash into long strips.

- Plunge them into a large pan of lightly salted water and cook for 2 minutes.

- Drain and refresh under the cold tap.

- Transfer to a serving dish and make sure there is an even mix of the two colours.

- If preferred, warm or reheat very briefly in a warming oven just before serving. However, the ribbons don't need to be served too hot.

Ingredients

400g courgettes

400g butternut squash, peeled

Equipment

wide-mouth peeler

CONSTABLE OF THE TOWER

In charge of the City's fortress is the Constable of the Tower. It is possibly the oldest office in the UK, dating from the 1070s when William the Conqueror built the Tower of London and installed his first Constable. It was a position of great prestige and wealth; even today it includes a promise from the Monarch that every ship or gallery coming to the City with wine will give the Constable a contribution from their cargo. The instructions are very specific, making sure that one gallon comes from the hold afore and behind the mast, presumably to ensure the captain does not hold back the good stuff. I am not sure whether any wine still enters this country via the Thames but sadly, although the ruling still stands, it is apparently no longer practised.

VEGETARIAN & VEGAN

AVOCADO & ORIENTAL VEGETABLE SUMMER ROLLS

With the influences of different cuisines from around the world, vegetarian and vegan dishes have become far more diverse. These Vietnamese-style summer rolls make a delicious starter or summer main course. They are also gluten-free, nutritious and vegan.

SERVES 6

Ingredients

500g oriental vegetables, such as beanshoots, peppers, carrots or mouli

1 red chilli, deseeded and finely chopped

1 bunch coriander, shredded

1 piece ginger, approx. 4cm, grated

2 limes, juice and zest

2 tbsp tamarind gluten-free soy sauce

6 Vietnamese rice paper wrappers

1 avocado, peeled and thinly sliced lengthways

18 mint leaves

To finish

Vegan Satay Sauce (see page 163)

coriander sprigs

• Cut all the vegetables into even-sized matchsticks and place in a large bowl.

• Add the chilli, coriander, grated ginger, lime juice and soy sauce. Mix well.

• Leave the vegetables to marinate for up to an hour.

• To make up the summer rolls, squeeze the excess moisture out of the vegetables with your fingers and divide into six even amounts.

• Soak the rice paper wrappers individually in a bowl of warm water for 20 seconds.

• Remove the wrappers from the water and lay out on a board.

• Place the vegetables, mint leaves and avocado slices in a line across the centre of the wrappers. Fold the sides in to seal, then roll tightly from one end to the other so the filling is totally enclosed.

• Cut each roll into three. Arrange on individual plates with the Vegan Satay Sauce and sprigs of coriander.

WINE WITH VEGETABLES

As a meat eater, I don't always think about pairing wines with vegetables. However, I am a vegetable lover and feel that sometimes I neglect our leafy friends! Winter vegetables, such as carrots or parsnips roasted with honey and cumin, or beetroot with goat's cheese and thyme, cry out for a warming Bordeaux-style red wine.

As spring emerges, new life appears, evenings get lighter and we enjoy wild garlic, purple sprouting broccoli and crisp asparagus.

It is then exciting to slurp back a full-bodied white wine, such as a Stellenbosch Chardonnay or an Australian Viognier, to complement my spring vegetables.

Summer is rosé time! But one must question whether rosé can be paired with all summer vegetables? I think the answer to this is a resounding... YES! Lettuces, cucumbers, radishes and tomatoes all demand a crisp Provence-style rosé. However, if you are looking for an alternative to rosé, you might also wish to try Picpoul de Pinet or

the ultimate summer white wine – Vermentino from Sardinia.

Lastly, we hit autumn, season of harvest and the ripe vegetables of a Mediterranean kitchen. Try ratatouille with fulsome red Pinot Noir; roasted aubergine, soy sauce and almonds with a white Rioja; or wild mushroom risotto with a bold Shiraz.

To sum up; when you are choosing your wine pairing with your vegetable dish, let the season guide you!
*Richard Gladwin,
Restaurateur and Wine Blogger*

SMOKED MOZZARELLA SOUFFLÉS

Smoked mozzarella is a great flavour for a soufflé, but I prefer it diluted by using some Cheddar as well. A twice-baked soufflé is highly versatile and can be adapted to make use of most things in your fridge, such as spinach, broccoli, bacon, ham, prawns or other cheeses. The secret of these foolproof soufflés is that they are first cooked in a bain-marie, then re-baked dry when ready to serve.

SERVES 6 (SMALL DISHES)

• Lightly butter six ramekin dishes. Melt the remaining butter in a heavy-based pan over a moderate heat. Stir in the self-raising flour and cook for 1 minute.

• Add the milk to the pan and bring back to the boil, stirring all the time to avoid lumps.

• Stir in both the cheeses, chives and season with salt and pepper.

• Take the pan off the heat, stir in the egg yolks and transfer the mixture to a large mixing bowl.

• In a separate bowl, whisk the egg white to soft peaks.

• Fold the egg whites into the cheese mixture then spoon into the ramekins.

• Place the ramekins in a roasting tin half-filled with water to make a bain-marie (see below).

• Bake the soufflés in a preheated oven at 180°C/gas mark 6 for 20–25 minutes until golden. Remove from the oven and leave to get cold – they will sink a little.

• When you want to serve the soufflés, turn them out of the ramekins. Line a baking tin with baking paper and place the soufflés in the tin. Re-bake at 200°C/gas mark 7 for 10–15 minutes until puffed up and perfect.

• Serve with heritage tomatoes, micro herbs and Hazelnut Dressing.

Ingredients

35g butter

30g self-raising flour

250ml milk

100g smoked mozzarella, grated

100g mature Cheddar cheese, grated

sprinkling of chives, finely chopped

salt and black pepper

2 eggs, separated

To serve

400g multicoloured heritage tomatoes, cut into interesting shapes

a small punnet of micro herbs

Hazelnut Dressing (see page 160)

BAIN-MARIE

The term 'bain-marie' literally means 'Mary's bath'. Mary was apparently an alchemist in the first century AD.

This is an age-old scientific and cookery technique that uses a heatproof bowl sitting over boiling water to gently melt or heat chemicals or food items without direct contact with the heat source.

WILD MUSHROOM ARANCINI

Just a few years ago, arancini were rare in the UK, but now they seem to appear on every menu and are prepared with a varying degree of expertise and success. The name comes from 'little oranges', which describes them perfectly. Traditional arancini, originally from Sicily, were rice balls filled with meat ragù or cheese, coated in crumbs and deep fried. In my opinion, too many recipes are based on using leftover risotto. Rich risottos have no place in Sicilian cooking, so although this recipe only uses vegan and gluten-free ingredients (and is therefore not authentic) we get closer to the traditional little orange snacks.

MAKES 18 BALLS (SERVES 6 AS A STARTER)

Ingredients

3 tbsp rapeseed oil

300g wild mushrooms, cleaned and broken into pieces

3 garlic cloves, crushed

3 thyme sprigs, leaves only, finely chopped

1 onion, finely diced

300g arborio rice

1 tsp salt

pinch of saffron

1 bay leaf

250ml vegetable stock, gluten free

250ml red wine (vegan)

200ml soya milk

400g breadcrumbs, gluten free

400ml oil, for deep-fat frying

Equipment

deep-fat fryer or sauté pan

• Heat the rapeseed oil in a heavy-based frying pan over a moderate heat and lightly fry the mushrooms, garlic and thyme for approximately 5 minutes.

• Remove the mushrooms from the pan and keep to one side. Sweat the onion in the same pan with the oil and juices. When the onion has softened, add the rice, salt, saffron and bay leaf. Stir for 2 minutes.

• Start to stir in the vegetable stock and red wine a little at a time until all the liquid is absorbed and the rice is sticky – it needs to cook for about 15 minutes.

• Add the wild mushrooms to the rice mixture and allow to cool.

• Take a tablespoon of the rice mixture at a time and roll into a ball in the palms of your hands. Place these in a shallow dish of soya milk and coat all over.

• Lift the rice balls out of the soya milk and roll them in a separate dish of breadcrumbs, again coating all over.

• Heat the cooking oil in a large heavy-based pan or deep-fat fryer set on a moderate heat. Using a slotted spoon, carefully lower the arancini into the hot oil and cook for approximately 5 minutes, until they are crisp and golden.

• Serve hot. I like to serve arancini with Romesco sauce (see page 40).

HERITAGE TOMATO & DATE TARTARE WITH ALMOND GAZPACHO

This is such an inspired and delicious starter, there is no way that you will want to reserve it just for vegan guests. It is a perfect beginning to a fine summer menu. The recipe was created by the Spanish contingent in our kitchens at Party Ingredients and you can see their Mediterranean influences. The sweetness and freshness of the tomatoes and dates contrasts beautifully with the mellow taste of garlic and the almond of the gazpacho.

SERVES 6

• Heat the olive oil in a small frying pan over a moderate heat and gently cook the onion to caramelize.

• Mix the tomatoes and dates with the cooked onion. Add the Mushroom Powder and chives, then season to taste with salt.

• Divide the mixture into six and press into the 8cm pastry cutter to mould each one into a tower. Chill until ready to serve.

• To make the almond gazpacho, blend the almonds, water and garlic in a liquidizer. With the motor still running, slowly add the oil, a little at a time.

• Finish with a splash of vinegar and season with salt. Chill until ready to serve.

• To plate the dish, place the tartare tower in the middle of the soup bowls. Pour the gazpacho carefully around.

• Garnish with the reserved chive stems, add droplets of Tomato Oil and a sprinkling of black onion seeds.

Ingredients

1 medium onion, finely diced

600g heritage tomatoes, deseeded and chopped

150g dates, chopped

1 tsp Mushroom Powder (see page 44)

1 bunch of chives, finely chopped, keeping a few stems in reserve

salt

olive oil, for frying

Tomato Oil (see page 159)

black onion seeds, for sprinkling

For the gazpacho

300g blanched almonds

750ml water

2 garlic cloves

600ml sunflower oil

white balsamic vinegar

salt

Equipment

8cm pastry cutter

AN OMELETTE TALE

There was a time in the City of London when the request for an alternative vegetarian dish was very rare. When such a thing was required the guest was usually presented with an omelette. An eminent and elderly City regular was by no means a vegetarian, but he did not like food to interfere with his consumption and enjoyment of fine wines. He would make a point of seeking me out in the Livery Hall kitchens prior to a major dinner to check on the menu. I can hear his barking military voice now asking, 'What are you dishing up this evening, Peter? Camel?'

Then, regardless of the delicacies on offer, he would insist we prepared him an omelette.

FENNEL & WATERMELON GRANITA

This is a perfect little 'inter-course' in the best possible way. Light, refreshing, stimulating and pleasing on the eye.

SERVES 6

Ingredients

1 kg watermelon

200g caster sugar

1 fennel bulb, cored and finely diced

1 lime, juice and zest, reserving the zest for garnish

fresh mint, finely chopped

salt and black pepper

• Scoop out the flesh of the watermelon into a sieve, retaining all the juice. Remove all the seeds.

• Finely dice about one-third of the melon flesh and set aside. Press the remaining melon flesh through the sieve.

• Place the sugar and melon juice in a medium pan over a low heat and stir until the sugar has melted.

• Add the diced fennel and lime juice, reserving the zest for garnish, then simmer for 5 minutes. The fennel should still have some crunch.

• Scoop out the fennel, set aside with the diced watermelon and transfer the liquid to a shallow container.

• Put a lid on the container and freeze for 2 hours.

• After 2 hours the liquid should have begun to freeze around the edges. Stir the frozen edges in with a fork and return to the freezer.

• Repeat this process two or three times until all the liquid has frozen into ice crystals.

• Place six glasses into the freezer half an hour before serving. Wet the glasses first if you want to create a frosted effect.

• Add the mint to the diced fennel and melon. Season to taste with a little salt and pepper.

• Place a spoonful of the diced mixture in the bottom of the glasses. Spoon some granita on top, finish with the lime zest and serve immediately.

COFFEE

Coffee first came to Europe in the mid-17th century and was variably described as 'most useless, since it serves neither for nourishment nor for debauchery' or as a 'pitiful drink – enough to bewitch a man and render him no use to women'.

LEEK TARTE FINE WITH CRANBERRY RELISH

We could call this dish a three-textured leek tart. Leeks are such a wonderful, wholesome, versatile vegetable it is worth taking time to prepare them – which can be done in multiple ways. The Leek Tarte Fine can be served as a starter or a main course and the simple cranberry relish sits very well alongside.

SERVES 6

• Begin by preparing the cranberry relish. Place all the ingredients in a food processor and pulse to roughly chop. Do not liquidize.

• Taste for seasoning and adjust as necessary. Store in the fridge.

• To make the leek tarts, cut 18 x 1cm oval leek discs on the diagonal. Wash the discs under cold water.

• Place the oval leek discs into a small pan of lightly salted boiling water and cook for 4 minutes. Drain, then brush with a little olive oil and set aside. Cut the remaining leeks into fine rings and wash well.

• Place the remaining olive oil and leek rings in a small pan over a moderate heat and fry until soft. Season to taste with salt, pepper and nutmeg.

• Place half of the fried leeks into a food processor and blitz to a purée. Once again, check the seasoning.

• Roll out the pastry onto a floured work surface. Using the 10cm pastry cutter, cut six discs out of the puff pastry and prick all over with a fork. Line a baking tray with baking paper and place the discs in the tray. Place another sheet of the paper on top. This will prevent the pastry bases rising out of shape.

• Bake the pastry discs in a preheated oven at 200°C/gas mark 7 for 15 minutes until crisp.

• Spread the leek purée on top of the pastry, then layer the fried leek rings on top.

• Heat the ribbed griddle pan until very hot and cook the reserved leek discs for 1 minute, pressing down to achieve charcoal rib marks. Place three leek discs on top of each tart.

• Reheat when ready to serve. Present the Tarte Fine with the cranberry relish, a dribble of Wild Garlic Oil and a sprinkle of Leek Ash.

Ingredients

750g leeks

2 tbsp olive oil

salt and black pepper

1 packet ready-roll puff pastry

For the cranberry relish

150g fresh cranberries

100g dried cranberries

100g walnuts

peel of 1 orange

2 tbsp Agave syrup

salt, black pepper and ground nutmeg

To finish

Wild Garlic Oil (see page 159)

Leek Ash (see page 45)

Equipment

10cm pastry cutter

ribbed griddle pan

'The mind, once stretched by a new idea, never returns to its original dimensions.'
Ralph Waldo Emerson

RED PEPPER & CHICKPEA PAKORAS WITH PEA & MINT PURÉE

One of the joys of working in an ethnically diverse kitchen is that we all learn from one another. The modern City's multicultural approach to eating provides a wonderful range of vegetarian and vegan possibilities. Indian, Middle Eastern and Asian cooking is full of exciting ingredients, dishes and techniques that we think are new and innovative but have in fact been around for thousands of years. These simple but delicious fried pakoras are a good example.

MAKES 18 PAKORAS (6 STARTER PORTIONS)

Ingredients

2 red peppers

240g canned chickpeas, drained and rinsed

1 red chilli, deseeded and finely chopped

½ bunch coriander

90g flour

1 tsp salt

1 tsp cumin

1 tsp mild curry powder

1 litre sunflower or rapeseed oil, for deep-fat frying and oiling

For the pea & mint purée

500g frozen peas

mint leaves

To finish

2 tbsp red wine vinegar

2 tbsp water

1 red onion, cut into strips

100g peashoots

pea powder, for sprinkling

Equipment

deep-fat fryer (optional)

- Brush oil onto the peppers and roast in a preheated oven at 180°C/gas mark 6 for 10 minutes.

- Carefully peel off the skins of the peppers and remove the core and seeds.

- Blend the chickpeas, red peppers, chilli, coriander, gram flour, salt and spices in a food processor.

- Heat the cooking oil in a large heavy-based pan or deep-fat fryer set on a moderate heat.

- When the oil begins to smoke, roll the pakora mixture into 6cm balls in the palm of your hands and carefully lower them into the hot oil.

- Cook for approximately 4 minutes until crisp and golden.

- Lift the pakora out of the oil onto kitchen paper. Keep warm or place on a tray to reheat when needed.

- Cook the peas in lightly salted boiling water for 5 minutes. Drain, transfer to the food processor, add the mint leaves and blitz until smooth.

- Heat the vinegar and water in a small pan over a low heat and cook the onion strips for 2 minutes. Leave to cool in the liquid.

- Reheat the pakoras and the pea purée, then arrange on individual plates with a topping of pickled red onion and pea shoots. Sprinkle with the pea powder.

'Do not allow yourself to be disheartened by any failure as long as you have done your best.'
Mother Teresa

BROAD BEAN HUMMUS KOFTE WITH LENTILS & TOMATO CONCASSE

A Middle Eastern kofte is normally minced lamb or beef moulded onto a skewer and cooked over a grill. This broad bean vegan version is a great substitute. Here we are serving the kofte with puy lentils, diced vegetables and a tomato concasse.

MAKES 12 (SERVES 6)

- Blitz the broad beans and chickpeas together in a food processor.

- Add the tahini, cumin, coriander, chickpea flour, salt and lemon juice. Blend again. You should have a thick, tacky paste; you can add a little more chickpea flour at this stage if the paste is too wet.

- Divide the mixture into 12 even amounts and carefully mould each onto the bamboo skewers to form a kofte. Roll individually in the sesame seeds and place onto a baking tray ready to bake or grill.

- To prepare the lentils, rinse under cold water then place in a pan of water over a moderate heat. Bring to the boil then add the diced vegetables.

- Simmer gently for 15 minutes.

- Drain the lentil mixture, season well with salt and pepper and keep warm.

- To prepare the tomato concasse, peel the tomatoes by first lightly scoring the skin into quarters. Place the tomatoes in a bowl, pour over boiling water, wait 1 minute, then transfer them to a bowl of cold water. Now peel off the skins with the tip of a paring knife.

- Fry the onion in a little oil over a moderate heat, season to taste and cook until soft.

- Deseed and dice the tomato and combine it in the pan with the hot onion. Add the red wine vinegar. Remove from the direct heat but keep warm.

- Drizzle the kofte with a little olive oil. Cook under a hot grill or bake in a preheated oven for 15 minutes at 200°C/gas mark 7.

- Serve with the lentil mixture, the tomato concasse, and a drizzle of Wild Garlic Oil.

Ingredients

300g cooked broad beans

300g canned chickpeas, drained and rinsed

1 tbsp tahini paste

2 tsp cumin

1 small bunch coriander, shredded

30g chickpea flour

1 tsp salt

juice of ½ a lemon

1 tbsp mixed black and white sesame seeds

olive oil, for frying and drizzling

For the lentils

150g puy lentils

1 carrot, diced

½ onion, diced

2 celery sticks, diced

salt and black pepper

For the tomato concasse

4 plum tomatoes

½ onion, finely chopped

1 tsp red wine vinegar

To finish

Wild Garlic Oil (see page 159)

Equipment

12 x 6in bamboo skewers

Extract from *The Glory of the Garden*

Our England is a garden that is full of stately views,
Of borders, beds and shrubberies and lawns and avenues,
With statues on the terraces and peacocks strutting by;
But the Glory of the Garden lies in more than meets the eye.
Rudyard Kipling

WILD HERB, LEMON & BUTTERNUT RISOTTO

My son Oliver is the Executive Chef of Gladwin Restaurants. He and his brothers (with a little guidance from dad) run a group of highly acclaimed eateries in London, based around Sussex produce and all things local and wild. Oliver is the master of foraged herbs and can take you to a London park to find pennywort, oak moss, three-cornered leeks, hairy bittercress and much more. There is nothing like a well-made risotto prepared just before serving as a vehicle for using wild herbs to best effect. It makes a delicious lunch or supper main course dish.

SERVES 4–6 (AS A MAIN COURSE)

Ingredients

2 butternut squash, peeled and chopped into cubes

3 tbsp sunflower oil

½ large white onion, finely chopped

1 garlic clove, crushed

350g arborio rice

1 tsp salt

250ml white wine

black pepper

a good bunch of herbs, such as pennywort, chervil, wood sorrel, wild garlic or leek cresses

1 lemon, juice and zest, reserving the zest

• Prepare a butternut purée by cooking the cubes of butternut squash in a pan of lightly salted water for 15 minutes. Drain, but save the cooking liquid.

• Place in a blender and liquidize the butternut squash until smooth.

• Transfer the butternut squash to a measuring jug and add water from the cooking to make up to 750ml.

• To cook the risotto, heat the oil in a large, open, heavy-based frying pan over a moderate heat and fry the onion and garlic until soft. Add the rice and salt to the pan and stir gently for 2 minutes – you will see the rice grains go opaque.

• Slowly stir in the white wine and lemon juice, reserving the zest, while continuing to cook.

• As the rice gently absorbs the liquid, stir in the butternut purée a ladle at a time.

• Stop cooking when the rice has swelled but still has a little bite to it. This takes approximately 15 minutes.

• Check the flavour and season with the black pepper.

• Stir in the herbs, add the lemon zest and serve immediately.

CHICORY, RED ONION & GOAT'S CHEESE TARTE TATIN

This main course upside-down tart will satisfy even the most ardent carnivore. It is innovative, wholesome and a lovely marriage of bitter, sweet and savoury flavours.

SERVES 4–6

- To make the pastry, place the flour, butter, goat's cheese, salt and cayenne in a food processor and pulse for just 2 seconds – it should look like coarse breadcrumbs.

- Add the water and pulse again.

- Turn the mixture out onto a lightly floured surface and kneed it into a ball. Wrap in clingfilm and chill in the fridge until required.

- To make the filling, heat the sugar in a small pan over a low heat and allow to melt and caramelize to a deep golden colour.

- Take the pan off the heat and add the vinegar. Stand well back as it will splutter. Season to taste with salt and pepper.

- Pour the hot caramel mixture into the bottom of the cake tin.

- Place a few strands of onion onto the caramel then place the halves of chicory, cut-side down. Press the vegetables down to fill all the space. Add a layer of goat's cheese and the rest of the red onion.

- Roll out the pastry on a floured surface into a 25cm circle.

- Cover the vegetables, goat's cheese and caramel with the pastry and tuck in the sides around the edge.

- Bake in a preheated oven at 180°C/gas mark 6 for 30 minutes until golden brown.

- Allow to cool for 5 minutes before using a small round-ended knife to turn the tart out and over.

- Reheat before serving, garnished with the strips of cooked red onion and the lamb's lettuce.

Ingredients

For the shortcrust pastry

160g plain flour

100g butter

100g dry goat's cheese

salt and cayenne pepper

1 tbsp water

For the filling

100g caster sugar

1 tsp red wine vinegar

salt and pepper

1 red onion, sliced

4 chicory, split lengthways

100g dry goat's cheese, crumbled

To finish

lightly cooked strips of red onion

lamb's lettuce

Equipment

20cm non-stick cake tin

FISH

HRH'S FISH PIE

Recipe contributed by HRH The Duchess of Cornwall

**CLARENCE HOUSE
LONDON SW1A 1BA**

My one big claim to fame is that The Duchess of Cornwall and I planted the millionth grape vine in Great Britain together at the 2017 South of England show. How many chefs can say that! I was the Chairman of The United Kingdom Vineyard Association at the time (now Wines of Great Britain) and the Duchess is its Royal Patron and President. The growth of the English wine industry is phenomenal and our ceremonial planting was the millionth vine in the ground that year alone. Additional planting is now running at nearly 2 million new vines each year. With all this in mind, I must recommend serving a crisp aromatic English white wine to accompany this dish. I am sure Her Royal Highness would approve.

SERVES 6

Ingredients

400g natural smoked haddock

400g salmon

400g pollock

400g seabass

600ml milk

bay leaf and black peppercorns

50g butter

50g plain flour

8 large Désirée potatoes, peeled and cooked for mashing

100g butter

1 egg yolk

4 eggs, soft boiled and cut into quarters

1 tbsp finely chopped parsley

1 tsp finely chopped dill

1 lemon, zest

pinch of grated nutmeg

salt and black pepper

• Cut all the fish into chunks and place in a large ovenproof casserole dish. Pour over 500ml of the milk. Add the bay leaf and peppercorns. Place a lid on top and cook in a preheated oven at 180°C/gas mark 6 for 30 minutes.

• Drain the cooking liquor from the fish through a sieve into a jug. Reserve the liquor and allow the fish to cool.

• Heat the butter in a heavy-based pan over a medium heat. Stir in the flour and cook for 1 minute. Stir in the fish cooking liquor a little at a time to form a smooth sauce. Season to taste with salt and pepper. If necessary, add a little extra milk or cream to make the volume up to 500ml.

• Mash the cooked potatoes with the butter, egg yolk, salt, pepper and the remaining 100ml of milk. This is best done while the potatoes are still hot.

• Lay the mixed fish in an ovenproof pie dish. Add a layer of the boiled eggs. Sprinkle with parsley, dill, lemon zest and nutmeg. Pour over the sauce then pipe the mashed potato in a thick layer on top.

• Bake in the oven at 190°C/gas mark 7 for 30 minutes.

BAKED COD & TAPENADE CRUST WITH SOFT POLENTA & PEPERONATA

All the lovely Italian elements to this dish are very versatile and can be used in other recipes. Tapenade is great as a canapé spooned onto a bread croûte; polenta is an excellent side for stews and poultry dishes; and peperonata is a staple in any Italian home to accompany pasta, steamed vegetables or grilled meats.

SERVES 6

- Take one-third of the black and green olives and chop them by hand. Set aside. Put the remaining olives and all the other tapenade ingredients in a food processor and blitz to a purée. Season to taste, although the anchovy should provide enough salt.

- To prepare the peperonata, heat the olive oil in a heavy-based pan over a low heat and fry the onion and garlic until soft but not browned.

- Stir in the strips of pepper and continue to cook gently for 15 minutes. Stir in the tomatoes and season well with salt and pepper. Keep warm.

- Lay the cod pieces out on a baking tray, lined with baking paper. Spread a layer of tapenade on each, scatter the chopped olives on top, then bake in a preheated oven at 190°C/gas mark 7 for 8–10 minutes.

- The art of a good soft polenta is to cook it just before serving. Traditional cornmeal requires about 40 minutes of cooking so I recommend using dried instant polenta.

- Put the milk and stock into a medium-sized pan over a moderate heat. Add in the instant polenta, season well and continue to stir and cook for 3 minutes. Remove from the heat and mix in the Parmesan.

- Rest the baked cod for just 3 or 4 minutes then serve with the polenta, peperonata and a generous helping of watercress.

Fact or Fiction?

It was Victorian historian E.A. Freeman who said that we need not believe that all 'legends are records of facts; but the existence of these legends is a very great fact'. Myths and facts are always intertwined in the history of a great city and out of the confusion come traditions and heritage.

Ingredients

6 x 120g pieces cod fillet

For the tapenade crust

60g pitted black olives

60g pitted green olives

2 tbsp capers

30g anchovy fillets (optional), drained

1 clove garlic

1 lemon, zest and juice

30ml olive oil

30g flat-leaf parsley

pepper

For the peperonata

3 tbsp olive oil

2 red onions, sliced into strips

1 garlic clove

2 red peppers, quartered, deseeded and cut into 5mm strips

1 yellow pepper, quartered, deseeded and cut into 5mm strips

250g peeled plum tomatoes, fresh or canned

salt and black pepper

For the polenta

200ml milk

200ml vegetable stock

50g instant polenta

50g grated Parmesan

To finish

1 bunch of watercress

THE FISHMONGERS' COMPANY TURBOT

Recipe contributed by Stefan Pini, Executive Head Chef, The Fishmongers' Company

The Fishmongers is one of the Great 12 Livery Companies residing in a magnificent Hall adjacent to London Bridge and, of course, very close to the old Billingsgate Market. They recently introduced a new award for Master Fishmonger, which is presented by the Company's Prime Warden, the Princess Royal. There can be no better institution to contribute a recipe for turbot. Since the Roman Empire, turbot has been highly valued as the King of Fish for its refined flavour and meaty texture. In Stefan Pini's recipe, the turbot is complemented by miniature crab cakes and cauliflower prepared two ways – it is a complete banquet dish.

SERVES 6

Ingredients

6 x 110g portions of turbot

100g butter

For the mini crab cakes

60g plain potatoes, cooked and mashed

120g white crab meat

juice of ½ lemon

100g plain flour

3 eggs, beaten

100g Panko breadcrumbs

oil, for cooking

salt and black pepper

For the caramelized cauliflower purée

1 cauliflower, roughly chopped

150g butter

20ml sherry vinegar

100ml water

For the cauliflower florets

1 cauliflower, cut into 12 half-florets

¼ tsp cumin seeds

¼ tsp fennel seeds

1 garlic clove, finely chopped

2 shallots, very thinly sliced

To finish

Wild Garlic Oil (see page 159)

12 sprigs of dill

• Begin by preparing the mini crab cakes. Combine the potato, crab, lemon juice and seasoning. Divide the mixture into 12 even cakes.

• Put the flour, eggs and breadcrumbs into separate bowls. Roll the crab cakes in flour, then egg, then breadcrumbs. Heat the oil in a heavy-based pan over a moderate heat and fry the crab cakes for 3 minutes, until golden brown, then set aside.

• Next, make the cauliflower purée. Melt 150g butter in a large pan over a medium heat until it starts to turn nut-brown in colour. Add the chopped cauliflower, turn down the heat and cook for 10 minutes until the cauliflower is well coloured and cooked through.

• Remove the pan from the heat and add the vinegar and water. Transfer to a food processor and blend until smooth. Season to taste and pass through a fine sieve.

• Blanch the cauliflower florets in a pan of lightly salted water for 40 seconds, drain and refresh under the cold tap.

• Heat 30g of the butter for the fish in a large heavy-based pan over a moderate heat. Season the turbot and cook it skin-side down for 3 minutes. Check the base of the fish is golden brown, then turn it over and add another 30g butter. Baste (spoon over the hot cooking juices) until the turbot is evenly cooked. Remove the fish from the pan and keep warm.

• Add the remaining butter and the cumin, fennel and garlic for the cauliflower florets to the pan and fry for a minute. Place the florets cut-side down and cook until tender. Finally, lightly fry the sliced shallots.

• Reheat the cauliflower purée and crab cakes. Assemble the dish and finish with the Wild Garlic Oil and fresh dill.

SALMON STEAMED IN BASIL LEAVES WITH BORLOTTI BEAN SALAD

This is a great summery fish main course. The salmon really takes on the aromatic essence and the sweetness of the basil, complemented by borlotti beans, cherry tomatoes and olives. We are serving the dish with a classic hollandaise sauce.

SERVES 6

- Set the salmon pieces out on a board and season to taste with a little salt and pepper.

- Melt the butter in a small pan over a moderate heat, dip the basil leaves in it and wrap a band of three basil leaves around each portion of fish.

- Carefully place the wrapped fish in a lightly buttered ovenproof dish. Add the remains of the bunch of basil around the sides.

- Place a good fitting lid on the dish or cover with a layer of greaseproof paper and aluminium foil. Set aside ready to cook.

- To make the salad, cook the fine beans in lightly salted boiling water for 5 minutes, Drain and refresh under the cold tap.

- Mix the cooked beans with the borlotti beans, tomatoes, olives, oil and lemon juice. Season to taste with salt and pepper.

- Cook the fish in a preheated oven at 190°C/gas mark 7 for 8–10 minutes. It will turn opaque on the outside but should still be pearly in the centre. Rest the fish for 5 minutes with the lid or cover on.

- Transfer the salmon to a serving platter, garnished with the wedges of lemon and flat leaf parsley. Serve with the bean salad and Hollandaise Sauce.

Ingredients

6 x 120g salmon fillets

1 bunch of basil (you will need 18 large leaves, picked off their stems)

125g melted butter

salt and black pepper

For the borlotti bean salad

250g fine green beans

240g canned borlotti beans, drained and rinsed

500g punnet mixed cherry tomatoes, halved

100g pitted black olives, halved

2 tbsp olive oil

juice of ½ lemon

salt and black pepper

To finish

2 lemons, cut into wedges

bunch of flat-leaf parsley

Hollandaise Sauce (see page 156)

DISRUPTED CONVIVIALITY

The greatest City dining catastrophe occurred in 1827 at the Lord Mayor's Banquet when a tremendous raft of oil lamps made in the shape of a huge anchor came crashing down on the top table, severely injuring the Lord Mayor and some of his principal guests.

To quote the somewhat understated Annual Register, 'the conviviality of the evening was disrupted.'

BILLINGSGATE SEAFOOD CURRY

Recipe contributed by C.J. Jackson, Principal and Chief Executive, Billingsgate Seafood School

The range and quantity of fish that passes through Billingsgate Fish Market on a daily basis is astonishing, and this recipe supplied by the market's own cookery school includes some of the great variety of fish available. We buy all our fish through the market and over the years have got to know some of the wonderful characters who work there.

SERVES 4

Ingredients

675g white fish fillet, such as pollock, hake or gurnard

250g clams, rinsed and closed

250g raw warm-water prawns, peeled and de-veined

2 squid tubes, thickly sliced

55g butter

2 onions, finely chopped

I green chilli, deseeded and finely chopped

3 garlic cloves, crushed

2 tsp fresh root ginger, peeled and grated

I tsp hot chilli powder

I tsp freshly grated turmeric

I tsp ground coriander

I tsp ground cumin

2 tbsp tamarind paste

6 tomatoes, peeled, deseeded and chopped

I tbsp tomato purée

410g canned coconut milk

salt and black pepper

coriander leaves, to garnish

• Carefully debone the white fish. Cut into 5cm pieces and set aside. Clean, prepare and check the other seafood ready for cooking.

• Melt the butter in a pan, add the onions and cook over a gentle heat for 20 minutes until soft and golden brown. Add the chilli, garlic and ginger to the pan and continue to cook for 3 minutes.

• Stir the chilli powder, turmeric, coriander, cumin and tamarind into the mixture and fry for 2 minutes. Stir in the tomatoes, tomato purée and coconut milk. Bring to the boil, then simmer for 5 minutes.

• Now add the white fish pieces, clams and prawns and cook over a gentle heat for 5 minutes until the fish is just cooked (it should be opaque). Stir in the squid for the last 30 seconds and cook until it has lost its translucency.

• Lift the fish from the cooking liquid into a serving dish and keep warm.

• Put the sauce back on a high heat and boil rapidly to reduce by one-third. Season to taste with salt and pepper.

• Pour the sauce back over the fish, garnish with a handful of coriander leaves and serve.

BILLINGSGATE FISH MARKET

Billingsgate Market was historically situated on Lower Thames Street in the City, but in 1982 it was relocated to the Isle of Dogs in East London. It is the largest indoor fish market in the UK and is still run by the City Corporation, but the freehold owner of the new site is the London Borough of Tower Hamlets. The market must make 'a gift of one fish per annum' to pay for its tenancy.

ROASTED MONKFISH IN IBÉRICO HAM & CHORIZO CRUMB

Monkfish is a wonderful meaty fish that makes an excellent partnership with strongly flavoured cured Spanish pork. This dish also works well as a main course and, as my son Richard would tell you, it provides a great chance to serve powerful red wine with fish. We are wrapping the fish in Ibérico ham and serving it with a white saffron butter sauce and the crunch of fried chorizo and breadcrumbs. To balance all these rich flavours, the monkfish sits on a bed of red and green cabbage.

SERVES 6

• Melt half the butter in a small pan over a moderate heat and season it well with salt and pepper. Coat the fish with butter on all sides but do not cook.

• Wrap a slice of ham around each piece of fish and place the wrapped fish on a baking tray ready to roast.

• Heat the duck fat in a pan over a moderate heat. Fry the chorizo until crisp, add the brioche breadcrumbs and fry until golden.

• Cook the red cabbage in a pan of lightly salted boiling water with the vinegar for 6 minutes. Drain well.

• Return the cabbage to the pan, add a tablespoon of redcurrant jelly and toss over the heat for 2 or 3 minutes. Keep warm.

• Cook the Savoy cabbage in the same way, but add the rest of the butter and the grated apple when cooked.

• Roast the monkfish in a preheated oven at 180°C/gas mark 6 for 6–8 minutes. Take the fish out of the oven, cover with foil and rest for 5 minutes before serving.

• Serve the fish with the red and green cabbages and the Saffron White Butter Sauce, sprinkled with a few chives.

Ingredients

40g butter

6 x 120g pieces monkfish tail

6 slices Ibérico ham

40g duck or goose fat

100g chorizo, finely diced

100g brioche breadcrumbs

450g red cabbage, shredded

1 tbsp vinegar

1 tbsp redcurrant jelly

450g Savoy cabbage, cored, inner leaves shredded

1 small apple, grated and coated in lemon juice

salt and black pepper

To serve

Saffron White Butter Sauce (see page 162)

a few chopped chives

'One cannot think well, love well, sleep well, if one has not dined well.'
Virginia Woolf

THE SKINNERS' COMPANY
THE OTHER DAY AT THEIR
ENTERTAINING OF GENERAL
MONK HAD TOOK DOWN THE
PARLIAMENT ARMS IN THEIR
HALL AND SET UP THE KING'S

Samuel Pepys 11th April 1660

SPICY GRILLED OYSTERS

Recipe contributed by Henry Harris, a Liveryman of the Worshipful Company Of Cooks

Henry Harris was, for many years, the chef patron of Racine restaurant in Knightsbridge. This was a genuine foodies' restaurant, now sadly closed. Henry chose this recipe to reflect the fact that oysters were very much a staple of the City of London, and pairing them with a spicy curried butter reflects the global nature and reach of the City today.

SERVES 3 TO 6

Ingredients

250g butter, softened

1 shallot, very finely chopped

1 heaped tsp Madras curry powder

small piece of fresh ginger, peeled

1 lemon, juice and zest

2 spring onions

18 oysters in the shell

salt and black pepper

¼ bunch of coriander leaves, to garnish

• Place a small amount of the butter in a small pan over a moderate heat. Cook the chopped shallot and curry powder for 5 minutes until soft.

• Place the remaining butter in a bowl and beat the shallot mixture into it. Season to taste with salt and pepper.

• Use a fine grater to grate in a little ginger together with the zest and juice of the lemon. Slice the spring onions into long fine strips and place in a bowl of cold water along with a few ice cubes. They will curl.

• Carefully open the oysters and place on a shallow roasting tin. Put a small spoonful of curried butter on top of each. Place under a hot grill for a few minutes until the butter melts and bubbles.

• Arrange the lightly cooked oysters on a platter, drain the spring onions and scatter over along with some coriander leaves.

'As I ate the oysters with their strong taste of the sea and their faint metallic taste that the cold white wine washed away, leaving only the sea taste and the succulent texture, and as I drank their cold liquid from each shell and washed it down with the crisp taste of the wine, I lost the empty feeling and began to be happy and to make plans.'

Ernest Hemingway

CRAB FLORENTINE

Recipe contributed by Rick Stein

Sir David and Lady Brewer are as close as you can get to City royalty. Lord Mayor in 2005 and then Lord-Lieutenant of Greater London and a Knight of the Order of the Garter, Sir David has been a great ambassador of the City of London for many years. He is also, however, very proud of his Cornish origins. For his own Lord Mayor's Banquet, he asked his good friend Rick Stein to come up with a special Cornish dish. It is simple, timeless and delicious and, once again with our grateful thanks, we are pleased to share it with you here.

SERVES 6

- Melt the unsalted butter in a heavy-based pan over a moderate heat. Add the spinach and toss until wilted, drain in a colander and cool.

- Make a bed of spinach in six china dishes, then top each dish with a pile of crabmeat.

- Infuse the milk with the onion, bay leaf and peppercorns by heating in a small pan, bringing up to a simmer then turning off the heat. Leave to infuse for 15 minutes, then sieve into a jug.

- To make the sauce, melt the butter in a pan over a moderate heat. Add the flour and cook for 1 minute, then whisk in the infused milk to make a sauce.

- Stir in the cream and Parmesan then cook for a further 5 minutes on a low heat. Remove from the heat, whisk in the egg yolk and check the seasoning.

- Spoon the sauce over the crab and spinach.

- Place the florentines under a hot grill for 5 minutes until golden brown.

- Garnish with paprika and serve immediately.

Ingredients

25g unsalted butter

400g spinach, picked and washed

500g fresh picked crab meat

450ml milk

1 small onion, studded with cloves

1 bay leaf

6 black peppercorns

For the Béchamel sauce

30g butter

30g flour

2 tbsp double cream

75g Parmesan, grated

1 egg yolk

sprinkling of paprika, to garnish

THE LORD MAYOR'S SHOW

Between the 15th and 19th centuries, the Lord Mayor's procession took place on both land and by river along the Thames but since 1857 it has gone by road alone. To this day, on a November Saturday morning, often in a cold wind or light drizzle, crowds of over half a million people line the route through the City to cheer and see the new Lord Mayor.

There is a splendid array of military bands, themed floats (still called floats from the time the show was on water), elegant open carriages and, finally, the sumptuous golden coach, which was built for just this purpose in 1757. The Lord Mayor enthusiastically stretches out of the window to 'present himself to the people of the City'. The show day ends with a magnificent firework display on the river by Blackfriars and the new Mayoralty has been launched.

PERSIAN SALT & SPICED SQUID

Recipe contributed by former Prime Minister Theresa May

If you want something done, ask a busy person. In the midst of the dreaded Brexit negotiations, Peter Estlin (Lord Mayor of London 2018/19) told the Prime Minister about this little book project over dinner and lo and behold this tasty recipe arrived just a couple of weeks later. To be fair, credit for the recipe itself must be given to Sabrina Ghayour, who can best be described as 'the golden girl of Persian cookery'. Thank you Sabrina for helping Theresa out with this particular challenge.

SERVES 6

Ingredients

750g squid

2 tbsp black peppercorns

70g cornflour

3 tbsp sea salt flakes

3 tsp ground cumin

2 tsp ground coriander

1 ½ tsp turmeric

500ml sunflower or rapeseed oil, for cooking

To finish

mizuna salad leaves

½ red pepper, deseeded and cut into strips

1 lime, cut into slices

Equipment

pestle and mortar

- Cut the squid into rings about 1cm thick. Pat dry with kitchen paper and set aside.

- Using a pestle and mortar, crush the peppercorns as best you can then add the salt and other spices and grind until evenly combined. It doesn't need to be a fine powder.

- Combine the cornflour with the salt and spices in a plastic bag and shake it to make sure it is evenly mixed.

- Add the squid to the bag and toss so it is evenly coated in the spiced flour. Do not handle the squid too much or it will wet the coating.

- Put the oil in a deep frying pan over a high heat. Bring up to a high temperature but turn down the heat when it begins to smoke.

- Shake off any excess spiced flour and fry the squid in batches for about 1–1 ½ minutes until golden and crispy. Using a slotted spoon, lift the squid out of the oil and onto kitchen paper.

- Arrange the salad leaves and red pepper on a serving platter and place the hot squid on top. Garnish with lime slices.

RED WINE WITH FISH

'Red wine with fish. Well, that should have told me something.' This is a quote from James Bond in the film *From Russia with Love*, when the bad guy is finally identified. From an early age I was taught that it is a social no-no to drink red wine with fish!

The fact is red wine can be delicious with fish. Delicate fish such as seabass, red mullet or bream are perfect cooked on a barbecue to create a smouldering chargrilled flavour, served with a simple wedge of lemon. The light vanilla oakiness from some lighter red wines plays beautifully with these dishes. Gamay from Beaujolais, cool-climate Pinot Noirs from Oregon or New Zealand and Côte de Nuits from northern Burgundy are all good complements.

Meatier fishes such as turbot, halibut and cod are more traditionally served with bigger, buttery sauces. The richness of the sauce can create a flavour-bridge to match the fullness of red wine. Earthier grape types such as Grenache and Mencía suit turbot well, and baked halibut or cod with wild mushrooms and Rioja Reserva are irresistible.

So going back to *From Russia with Love*, Dover sole, butter sauce and Chianti can go together. James Bond was wrong!
Richard Gladwin, Restaurateur and Wine Blogger

LOBSTER THERMIDOR

The original lobster thermidor was a creation of Escoffier in Paris in around 1880. It is timeless, celebratory and indulgent. We have served it for many great State occasions in the City. This recipe is a thermidor like no other and I must warn you the whole dish is quite elaborate, using several preparations detailed elsewhere in this book. Instead of filling lobster shells with the creamy lobster mixture, the dish is partly deconstructed and a scooped-out courgette is used as the principal 'vessel'. There are then the additions of umami-flavoured seaweed aïoli, the tang of balsamic pearls, the richness of a seafood bisque and, finally, the colour and freshness of green herbs.

SERVES 6

• Cut the courgettes into two lengthways, trim off the ends and scoop out the insides to make a boat.

• Blanch the courgettes in a large pan of lightly salted boiling water for 2 minutes. Drain and refresh. Place cut-side down on kitchen paper to thoroughly drain.

• Break open the lobster shells and remove all the meat, being careful to keep the tails whole.

• Place the shells in a medium-sized pan together with some herbs. Cover with water, bring to the boil then simmer for 20 minutes. Sieve the liquid into a jug and discard the shells and herbs. This will be the stock for the thermidor sauce and bisque.

• Slice nine discs of lobster from each tail (18 in total), lightly season to taste with salt and pepper and keep covered in the fridge until needed. Roughly chop all the remaining meat and set aside.

• Place the butter and shallot in a heavy-based pan over a moderate heat. Cook for 2 minutes, stir in the flour and cook for a further 2 minutes.

• Slowly stir in the lobster stock, wine, cream and lemon vinegar. Bring to the boil then season to taste with mustard powder, Tabasco and salt and pepper.

• Remove from the heat and stir in the chopped lobster meat. Fill the courgette boats with the mixture, sprinkle with Parmesan and place on a baking tray. Keep in the fridge until ready to bake.

• Prepare the aïoli by blending the mayonnaise with powdered nori leaf and crushed garlic.

• Heat up the Seafood Bisque and assemble all the other elements of the dish, if you are using them.

• Bake the filled courgettes in a preheated oven at 200°C/gas mark 7 for 5 minutes.

• Arrange the cold lobster discs, aïoli and Balsamic Pearls on individual plates. Place the baked courgette in the middle. Spoon over the Seafood Bisque, drizzle with Salsa Verde and finish with red amaranth cress.

Ingredients

3 large courgettes

2 x 1.2kg lobsters, cooked

a handful of fresh tarragon, chives and parsley

20g butter

1 small shallot, finely diced

20g flour

100ml lobster stock, from the lobster shells

2 tbsp white wine

50ml cream

1 tsp lemon vinegar or lemon juice

a little English mustard powder

a few drops of Tabasco

salt and pepper

30g grated Parmesan, for sprinkling

For the seaweed aïoli

3 tbsp Mayonnaise (see page 51)

½ sheet nori leaf (sushi wrapper), blitzed to a powder

1 small garlic clove, crushed

To finish

Seafood Bisque (see page 72)

Balsamic Pearls (see page 39)

Salsa Verde (see page 164)

red amaranth cress

MEAT

FILLET OF BEEF WELLINGTON

Unfortunately, or fortunately, depending on whether you are the diner or the cook, the catering company that I co-founded, Party Ingredients, has a reputation for Beef Wellington cooked perfectly pink when carved at the moment of serving. It is a wonderful celebratory dish, but can be just a little stressful for the poor old chef when ordered for 800 guests.

SERVES 6–8

Ingredients

1–1.5kg beef fillet

500g block puff pastry

1 egg, salted and lightly beaten

salt and black pepper

For the mushroom duxelles

55g butter

500g field or wild mushrooms, finely chopped

1 garlic clove, crushed

1 tbsp parsley, finely chopped

To garnish

salad leaves

• Season the beef with salt and pepper. Place a heavy-based roasting tin or griddle plate directly over a high heat and when it is very hot, sear the fillet, rolling it onto all sides.

• Immediately transfer to a preheated oven and roast for 10 minutes at 220°C/gas mark 9.

• Remove the beef from the oven and allow to cool.

• To make the mushroom duxelles, melt the butter in a pan and sweat the mushrooms over a low heat with the garlic until they are soft. Season well, mix in the parsley, then leave to cool.

• When cool, place the mixture on a tea towel and squeeze out all the juice. You can save the juice to add to your sauce (see Good Gravy on page 167).

• On a floured work surface, roll the pastry out to an even rectangle approximately 40 x 30cm (big enough to completely wrap the beef in). Trim to size and save the pastry offcuts to decorate.

• Spread the duxelles down the centre of the pastry lengthways, to the same size as the fillet. Place the beef on top.

• Fold the pastry over the meat and seal with an overlap by brushing with beaten egg. Repeat with the ends of the pastry, folding them up and sealing.

• Turn the whole parcel over so the joins are on the underside.

• Use the pastry offcuts to decorate the top of the Wellington with a lattice.

• Brush with the rest of the beaten egg, then place on a baking sheet lined with baking paper. Refrigerate until ready to cook.

• Cook in a preheated oven at 180°C/gas mark 6 for 25–30 minutes until golden brown.

• Carve the Wellington at the table, garnished with salad leaves.

• I like to serve the Wellington with Sauce Béarnaise (see page 156) or a flavoursome mushroom jus (see Jus & Reductions, page 167).

'I did not say that this meat was tough. I just said I didn't see the horse that usually stands outside.'
W.C. Fields

STEAK & KIDNEY PUDDING

This recipe was contributed to the first *City of London Cookbook* by Sir Terence Conran

No City cookbook would be complete without the inclusion of a steak and kidney pudding recipe. Forget about the healthy eating and diet – this is the dish that everyone who has ever worked or visited the City assumes that plump businessmen in bowler hats eat on a daily basis! It is a delicious thing to have once in a blue moon. Perhaps introduce a bit of balance by having a salad starter and fresh fruit for dessert.

SERVES 6–8

• Roll the steak in seasoned flour. Place a heavy-based pan on a high heat, melt the butter and sear the steak until brown on all sides. Transfer to a deep roasting tin.

• Heat the onion, Guinness and Worcestershire sauce in a saucepan over a moderate heat and boil to reduce by two-thirds.

• Pour the reduced mixture over the meat then add the bay leaf, thyme and stock. Cover with a lid or foil and place in the oven at 150°C/gas mark 4.

• Place the kidneys in a pan, cover with water and bring to the boil. Pour off the water and leave the kidneys to one side.

• When the steak has been cooking for 1½ hours, add the kidneys to the mixture and cook for a further 1½ hours until tender. Remove the steak and kidney mix from the oven and chill.

• To make the pastry, place the dry ingredients in a mixing bowl, add the eggs and enough cold water to form a dough. Divide the pastry into two balls, one twice the size of the other, and roll out on a floured work surface into circles 6mm thick.

• Grease a china pudding bowl then line it with the larger disc of pastry. Spoon in the meats, top up with the cooking liquid, saving the excess as gravy to serve separately.

• Lay the other disc of pastry over the top and pinch the pastry lid and base together to seal.

• Cover with a disc of oiled greaseproof paper and a cloth tied securely with string. The pudding can then be kept in the fridge until needed.

• Place the pudding bowl into a pan and pour water around the sides. Bring up to the boil then steam for 2 hours, regularly topping up the water. The pan must not boil dry.

• Serve the pudding with creamy mashed potato, some old-fashioned vegetables, such as carrots, leeks, cauliflower or red cabbage, and plenty of extra gravy.

Ingredients

1.5kg chuck steak, diced into 2.5cm cubes

100g flour, seasoned

20g butter

1 onion, sliced

100ml Guinness

2 tbsp Worcestershire sauce

1 bay leaf

1 thyme sprig

500ml beef stock

700g ox kidney, diced, core removed

salt and black pepper

oil, for greasing

Suet pastry

500g plain flour

250g suet

1 tsp baking powder

pinch of salt

2 eggs, beaten

Equipment

2 litre china pudding bowl

an old napkin or piece of cloth and string to cover

The sin of gluttony: 'Let it be said that of all the deadly sins that mankind may commit, the fifth appears to be the one that least troubles his conscience and causes him the least remorse.'
Grimod de la Reynière

LOIN OF HIGHLAND VENISON WITH TUSCAN WINE & DARK CHOCOLATE SAUCE

Like so many seemingly contemporary dishes, this recipe is based on classic pairings. The sweet citrus and aniseed flavours of the marmalade make a lovely contrast to the lean tender meat, and the Tuscan red wine sauce enriched with dark chocolate is the perfect companion. We have also used a pastry croustade to hold the marmalade and provide an element of carbohydrate in place of potatoes.

SERVES 6

Ingredients

1 kg loin of venison, trimmed

50cl Tuscan red wine, such as Chianti

1 onion, roughly chopped

1 lemon, cut into slices

2 bay leaves

2 sprigs of thyme

salt

1 tsp juniper berries

1 tsp peppercorns

1 tsp ground mixed spice

300ml chicken stock

1 tbsp dark brown sugar

1 tsp Dijon mustard

50g dark chocolate, grated

For the winter vegetables

200g baby beetroot, halved

300g chantenay carrots

300g cauliflower, cut into florets

200g winter greens, destemmed and washed

salt and black pepper

For the croustade

250g block puff pastry

1 egg, beaten with a little salt

Fennel & Kumquat Marmalade (see page 52)

mint sprigs, to garnish

Equipment

cast-iron griddle plate

• Marinate the venison overnight with the Tuscan wine, onion, lemon, bay, thyme and salt.

• Place a cast-iron griddle plate over a high heat and allow it to get very hot. Lift the meat out of the marinade and sear it on all sides then place in a roasting tin ready to cook.

• Transfer the marinade to a pan, add the juniper berries, peppercorns and mixed spice. Bring to the boil and simmer until it reduces by half. Strain the liquid into another pan, add the chicken stock, sugar and mustard. Again allow the liquid to reduce a little and test for seasoning. Set aside, ready to reheat when needed.

• To prepare the croustade, roll out the puff pastry on a floured work surface to approximately 6mm thickness, then neatly cut diamonds to approximately 8 x 4cm. Score a smaller diamond inside the edge without cutting all the way through. Transfer the pastry diamonds to an oiled baking sheet, brush with egg wash and bake in a preheated oven at 190°C/gas mark 7 for 12 minutes.

• Remove from the oven and allow to cool. With the tip of a sharp knife, lift out the centre piece of pastry along the score lines and hollow out to leave a neat pastry case. Fill these with Kumquat & Fennel Marmalade and place in a low oven to warm through.

• Cook the mix of winter vegetables in a large pan of lightly salted boiling water. Start with the hardest (the beetroot), then add the carrots, the cauliflower and finally the winter greens. Keep warm.

• Roast the venison loin as briefly as you dare. A preheated oven set at 220°C/gas mark 9 for 8 minutes should be enough, but then rest the meat in a low oven or warming cabinet for 10 minutes to make sure the heat has gone through the rare meat.

• Reheat the sauce and whisk in the grated chocolate.

• Carve the venison and serve with the winter vegetables, Fennel & Kumquat Marmalade croustade, the Tuscan wine sauce and a mint sprig to garnish.

GRILLED LAMB BROCHETTES WITH PISTACHIO, HONEY & WARM SPICES

We are extremely fortunate in this country – and in the City of London in particular – that we can eat a vast spectrum of food with influences from all over the world. Several years ago we worked with a charming young chef known simply by the name of Mo. He was hard working and humble, but immensely proud of his Persian origins. If we used ingredients or seasonings from the Middle East he would immediately take the dish as his own and double his already considerable enthusiasm.

SERVES 6

- Cut the lamb into 24 even-sized pieces. Toss in a bowl with the olive oil, lime juice, sumac, cinnamon, saffron and salt and pepper. Leave in the fridge to marinate for 2 hours or more.

- Thread the lamb and dates alternately onto the bamboo skewers.

- Mix the pistachios and honey and season with black pepper. Drizzle some of this mixture onto the lamb.

- Prepare the raita by halving and deseeding the cucumber, then grate it on the largest holes of a box grater. Mix with the yoghurt, cumin, shredded mint, seasoning and pomegranate seeds.

- Either grill the lamb brochettes on a barbecue or roast in a preheated oven at 225°C/gas mark 10 for 6–8 minutes.

- To make the courgette ribbons, use the wide-mouth peeler to cut the courgettes into long strips.

- Plunge them into a large pan of lightly salted water and cook for 2 minutes. Drain and refresh under the cold tap.

- Finish the brochettes with an extra coating of the pistachios and honey and serve with the courgette ribbons and cucumber raita, garnished with extra mint and pomegranate.

'If it has four legs and it's not a table, eat it.'
Cantonese saying

Ingredients

3 x lamb loin fillets

2 tbsp olive oil

1 lime, zest and juice

½ tsp sumac

½ tsp cinnamon

pinch of saffron

12 dates, stoned and halved

50g green pistachio nuts, chopped

2 tbsp runny honey

salt and black pepper

For the raita

1 cucumber, peeled

400g Greek yoghurt

1 tsp cumin seeds

fresh mint, leaves picked off and shredded, with extra to garnish

pomegranate seeds, with extra to garnish

salt and black pepper

To finish

800g courgettes

Equipment

6 x 20cm bamboo skewers

wide-mouth peeler

MOROCCAN LAMB WITH APRICOTS, CHICKPEAS, CUMIN & FENNEL SEEDS

If you have ever visited Marrakesh, you will know about the ever-present aroma of warm spices and charring meat that makes you feel instantly hungry. And if you can find somewhere to escape the frenetic bustle of a city that never sleeps – and can find a colourful embroidered cushion to lounge upon – indulge in a lamb tagine. The City of London is a very different place, but perhaps this dish will capture some of the exotic heat of North Africa.

SERVES 6

Ingredients

1 kg boned leg of lamb, cut into pieces

2 tsp ras el hanout

1 tsp ground cumin

1 tsp fennel seeds

100ml olive oil

1 large onion, sliced

2 tbsp plain flour

2 tbsp tomato purée

500ml lamb stock

1 cinnamon stick

100g dried apricots, cut in half

2 sweet potatoes, peeled and cubed

1 red pepper, quartered, deseeded and cut into strips

1 aubergine, cored and cubed

400g canned chickpeas, drained and rinsed

salt and pepper

coriander leaves, to garnish

• In a bowl, toss the lamb in the ras el hanout, cumin, fennel seeds and salt and pepper to coat well.

• Place 3 tablespoons of the oil in a large casserole dish over a moderate heat. Sear the lamb pieces on all sides. Lift out and set aside.

• Add another 3 tablespoons of the oil to the casserole and gently fry the onion. Once the onion has softened, return the meat to the dish, add the flour and cook for a further 2 minutes.

• Add the tomato purée and lamb stock, bring gently to the boil, pop in the cinnamon stick and dried apricots. Place a lid on top and simmer gently for 1 ½ hours until tender.

• Meanwhile put the remaining oil in a frying pan over a moderate heat and fry the sweet potatoes, red pepper and aubergine.

• Lightly stir the fried vegetables, cooking juices and the chickpeas into the casserole. Replace the lid and cook for a further 15 minutes.

• Garnish the dish with fresh coriander leaves.

• I like to serve this dish with Cauliflower & Romanesco Couscous (see page 81).

WINE AND RED MEAT PAIRINGS

When I finished school, I travelled to New Zealand to learn more about wine. I was fortunate enough to get a job at a prominent New Zealand Cellar Door where the manager took me under her wing to teach me a thing or two about wine pairings. One thing I will always remember – Merlot = steak, so get selling the Merlot! Full bodied, tobacco, oaked, blackberry, leathery red wine with a grilled Angus rump is the most classic of wine pairings.

However, you can get more adventurous than this. At one end of the spectrum you may serve Roe Deer Carpaccio with a zesty fresh Gamay or even a lighter style of Pinot Noir. For a summery Ibérico pork salad I would suggest going for a bolder style of white wine, such as Chardonnay or Riesling.

Somewhere in the middle, we have rack of lamb or beef fillet – where you should consider a fruity style of red wine from South America or Italy.

Robust lamb or venison casseroles or roasted joints call for a Bordeaux or the great wines from the Rhône Valley.

A general guide is the richer the dish, the heavier the wine, but it must not be a weight-lifting competition – 'complementing' is the watchword. *Richard Gladwin, Restaurateur and Wine Blogger*

GUINEA FOWL WITH WOOD PIGEON & ELDERBERRIES

After an amazing trip to the African savanna when our children were small, it was essential that a flock of guinea fowl came to live with us at Nutbourne to keep the memories of the holiday alive. These were wild and beautiful birds, but alas, they did not understand the perils of English foxes and within just a few short weeks had all become dinner for our cunning bushy-tailed friends. You can't blame the foxes; guinea fowl are delicious to eat – a flavour somewhere between a chicken and a pheasant. The wood pigeon in this recipe gives a richness to the dish and the foraged elderberries add a perfect contrasting tang.

SERVES 6

- Place the oil in a heavy-based pan over a high heat and sear the guinea fowl on both sides. Lift out and set aside.

- Turn down the heat and fry the onions and beetroot until soft. Add the pork and wood pigeon. Add the sugar and vinegar and season to taste with salt and pepper. Cook through for 5 minutes.

- Remove from the heat and stir in the breadcrumbs.

- Cut a pocket into each breast and fill with the wood pigeon mixture. Stretch out the bacon rashers on a board and tightly wrap these round the guinea fowl. Place in an oiled roasting tin ready to cook.

- Roast the guinea fowl in a preheated oven at 180°C/gas mark 6 for 15–20 minutes.

- Lift the guinea fowl out of the roasting tin and keep warm. Place the tin over a high heat, add the stock, wine and thyme. Bring to the boil then add the elderberries to it.

- Cut the breasts in half on an angle, arrange on individual plates and spoon the jus over.

- Serve this dish with the Parsnip, Sweet Potato & Aubergine Dauphinoise and some steamed spinach.

Ingredients

2 tbsp rapeseed oil, plus extra for oiling

6 guinea fowl breasts, boned out

1 red onion, finely chopped

1 cooked beetroot (not pickled), grated

100g minced pork

2 wood pigeon breasts, finely chopped

1 tsp demerara sugar

½ tsp red wine vinegar

1 tbsp dried breadcrumbs

6 rashers of bacon

500ml stock

200ml wine

thyme sprigs

30g elderberries

salt and black pepper

To serve

Parsnip, Sweet Potato & Aubergine Dauphinoise (see page 86)

steamed spinach

THE SWAN FEAST

The Vintners' Company is one of two Livery Companies in the City of London that have ancient rights to own and therefore eat swan. Every July, 'Swan Upping' takes place on the upper reaches of the River Thames when Liverymen mark the swans and give new cygnets a health check.

The Company also hosts an annual Swan Feast; however, these days no one actually eats swan.

Thirty plus years ago, when I used to cook for The Vintners' Company, a Swan Upper (a man employed to care for swans on the river) arrived at our kitchen door with a knotted sack containing two young cygnets that had collided with overhead

electricity cables near Henley-on-Thames. We were obliged to pluck, draw and roast the birds, then strip off the flesh to use as an authentic contribution to the Swan Feast dinner. The swans themselves cooked away a lot of fat, leaving dark, rather sinewy meat, indistinguishable from an undernourished goose. Not to be recommended.

PARTRIDGE BREASTS & DAMSON WRAPPED IN KING CABBAGE

Partridge are probably my favourite game birds. They are delicate, flavoursome but not too gamey and, when cooked with care, mouthwateringly tender. In this recipe we are wrapping them in cabbage leaves with a tart damson stuffing. This keeps them moist and juicy, but you must still be very careful not to overcook them. A partridge breast can be served pink.

SERVES 6

Ingredients

6 whole partridges

varied mix of onion, celery and carrot, roughly chopped

2 bay leaves

salt and black peppercorns

sage sprigs

100ml Manzanilla sherry and 1 tbsp sherry vinegar

2 tsp honey

3 parsnips, peeled

1 tsp arrowroot

oil, for frying

For the damson stuffing

12 king cabbage leaves

200g pitted damsons, diced

2 heaped tbsp redcurrant jelly

3 sage leaves, shredded

1 slice toast, in crumbs

salt and black pepper

To finish

Carrot & Orange Purée (see page 85)

chervil, to garnish

Equipment

wide-mouth peeler

- Carefully cut the breasts from the partridges and set aside. Place the carcasses in a large pan, cover with water, add onion, celery, carrots, bay, peppercorns, salt and sage sprigs. Bring to the boil then turn down to simmer and reduce the liquid for 2 hours.

- Pour the stock through a sieve into a small pan. Discard the carcasses and other ingredients. Add the sherry vinegar and honey. Boil rapidly for 5 minutes to reduce the sherry. Check the seasoning and allow to cool until needed.

- Prepare the parsnip shards by cutting long strips with a wide-mouth peeler. Fry or deep-fry until golden. Dry off any excess oil on kitchen paper, then place on a baking tin.

- Blanch the cabbage leaves by plunging them into boiling water then immediately refreshing them under the cold tap. Lay them out on a tea towel to dry.

- Toss the damsons in a small pan over a moderate heat and boil off any excess liquid. Add the redcurrant jelly, salt, pepper and sage. Remove from the heat and stir in the toasted crumbs to bind the mixture.

- Make a patty of the damson stuffing in your hands, place on top of each partridge breast and wrap in a cabbage leaf. Arrange the breasts in a shallow casserole dish. Add a little of the jus and cover with a lid.

- Cook in a preheated oven at 180°C/gas mark 6 for 12–15 minutes. While the breasts are cooking, reheat the sherry reduction, stir arrowroot and water together in a cup and mix this into the boiling liquid to thicken. Reheat the parsnips.

- Rest the breasts for no more than 5 minutes, then assemble the dish. Serve the breasts with the reduction and the Carrot & Orange Purée, garnished with chervil.

THE SWAN SONG

Like The Vintners' Company, The Dyers' Company also has Royal permission to own swans. They too help look after the birds on the River Thames and celebrate their special status with a grand feast. I have had the privilege to cook for this occasion, which involves the chef parading a stuffed swan round the dining room to the musical accompaniment of a magnificent 'Swan Song'.

Look up, my Masters,
mark my words,
and hear what we shall sing ye.

And Liv'ry men all,
both great and small,
now mark what they do bring ye.

A swan,
A swan,
An off'ring fair they bear.
A vem nobilem nunc cantamus.

POACHED CHICKEN WITH MUSHROOMS, LEEK & COURGETTE FLOWER

This is a delightful, light, summery dish, full of flavour and style. The chicken is poached in a seal of clingfilm, similar to the principle of sous vide (vacuum sealing and slow cooking in a water bath). This holds all the essence and moisture inside, making the meat extremely tender. We have presented the dish with a Stuffed Courgette Flower and a Tarragon White Butter Sauce, but to be really healthy you could substitute the butter sauce for a salsa.

SERVES 6

• Remove any skin from the chicken breasts and 'butterfly' by making a horizontal cut and opening out the meat like a book.

• Soak the trompette mushrooms in hot water to rehydrate for approximately 15 minutes.

• Peel three long leaves off the leek, cut these into strips lengthways and reserve.

• Finely shred the rest of the leek. Heat a little oil in a small pan and sweat until fully cooked. Lift out the leek, then lightly fry the girolles. Set aside to garnish the dish.

• Squeeze any excess moisture from the trompettes and mix with the cooked leek. Season to taste.

• Spread the shredded leek and mushroom in a line across the middle of each chicken breast. Roll into a tight cylinder. Wind a long ribbon of the leek leaves around the outside of the cylinder then wrap tightly in clingfilm. Tie knots at each end of the clingfilm to seal.

• Prepare the Stuffed Courgette Flowers, but for this dish I recommend a filling of cooked rice, peas and red pepper inside the flower petals.

• Prepare the Tarragon White Butter Sauce.

• Heat the chicken stock in a large pan over a moderate heat. Submerge the chicken breast cylinders in the stock and place a small saucepan lid (that fits inside the pan) on top to weigh them down. Poach for 8 minutes.

• Lift the chicken out of the pan and remove the clingfilm. Slice each cylinder in half and serve with the Stuffed Courgette Flowers, Tarragon White Butter Sauce and a scattering of the girolle mushrooms.

Ingredients

6 x corn-fed chicken breasts, boneless

30g dried trompette mushrooms

1 leek

60g girolle mushrooms

1 litre chicken stock

6 Stuffed Courgette Flowers (see page 83)

150g cooked arborio rice

40g cooked peas

½ red pepper, finely diced

160ml Tarragon White Butter Sauce (see page 162)

salt and black pepper

a little olive oil, for cooking

SMITHFIELD MARKET

Smithfield is the oldest London market, still situated where beasts were brought for slaughter as early as the 10th century. When I met a leading trader he was fiercely proud of his market's heritage and place in the City's history.

There has recently been a major internal modernization and today Smithfield trades in a huge range of products and specialist meats from all over the world.

The quaint Victorian setting is part of the Square Mile that we love – long may it be preserved.

BARBECUED PORK CHOPS WITH AVOCADO & WALNUT SALSA

The Square Mile is not renowned for its barbecue cooking but believe me, it does exist. There are hidden gardens, terraces and balconies that occasionally come into their own on a hot summer's evening. We all need to move on from the inevitable burgers, sausages and chicken pieces. I hope these pork chops might set you on a voyage of inspired barbecue cooking.

SERVES 6

Ingredients

6 x 180g pork chops

125ml dark soy sauce

2 garlic cloves, crushed

2 tsp ground ginger

1/2 tsp cayenne pepper

2 tbsp demerara sugar

For the walnut salsa

2 avocados, not too ripe

juice of 1 lime

30ml olive oil

1 red pepper, finely diced

1 fresh chilli, finely diced

1 small red onion, finely diced

80g walnuts, shelled and chopped

50g sultanas

small bunch of dill, chopped

salt and black pepper

To finish

3 peaches, quartered, stoned and fanned

salad leaves and continental parsley

• Marinate the pork chops for a minimum of 2 hours in a mixture of the soy sauce, garlic, ginger, cayenne and sugar.

• To prepare the salsa, peel, stone and chop the avocado. Place in a mixing bowl and coat in lime juice to preserve the colour, then add the olive oil.

• Add the pepper, chilli and onion to the avocado together with the walnuts, sultanas and dill. Gently mix and season with salt and pepper.

• Transfer the salsa to a serving dish. Place in the fridge for an hour or so to combine the flavours.

• Light a hot barbecue, but be patient and wait until the flames are gone and you have glowing embers to cook on. Grill the pork chops on both sides, basting them with the marinade.

• Do the same with the peach pieces. Then arrange on a serving platter lined with some colourful salad leaves and parsley.

• I like to serve this dish with Red Quinoa, Baby Spinach, Orange & Feta Salad (see page 80).

THE BOAR'S HEAD CEREMONY

On a chilly December afternoon in Bartholomew's Close behind Bart's hospital, a group of robed gentlemen, a military band and a mounted police escort assemble to parade a fanciful representation of a boar's head through the City of London. To the astonishment and amusement of passers-by, The Butchers' Company are repeating a 650-year-old ceremony of presenting a boar's head to the Lord Mayor. They do this in commemoration of a charter in 1343 granting them a parcel of land near Fleet Street on which to slaughter their beasts. On arrival at the Mansion House the false head is replaced by a stuffed boar's head and the Lord Mayor and assembled company are offered a small slice.

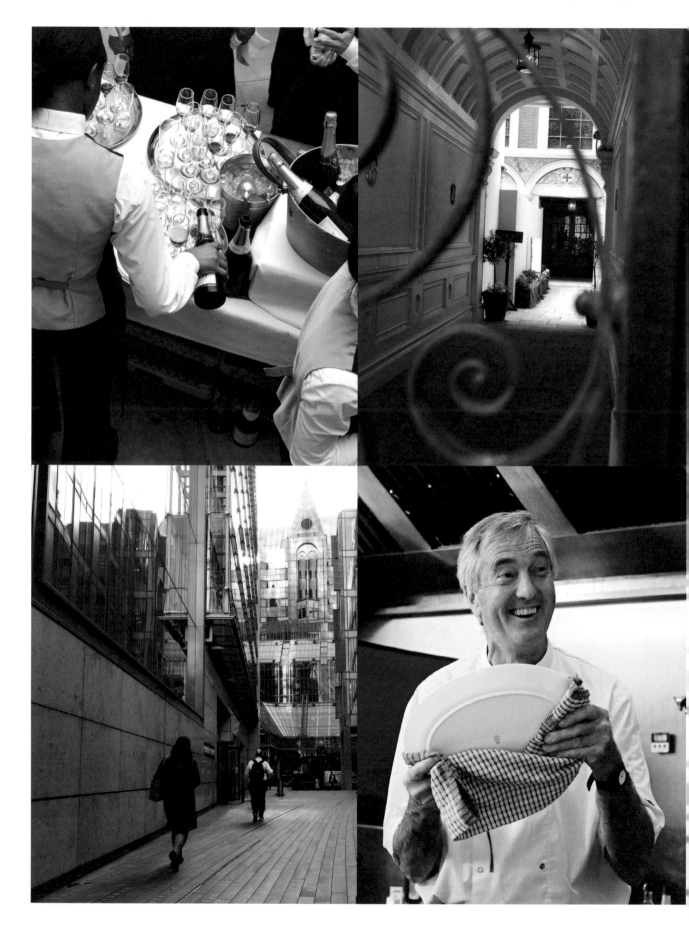

EMULSIONS, INFUSIONS & GOOD GRAVY

BASIC HOLLANDAISE & OTHER EMULSIONS

Hollandaise is a wonderful emulsion combining egg and butter – it adds richness and flavour to so many otherwise bland dishes and keeps well in the fridge, ready to use. This easy-to-make base recipe is ideal to serve with salmon, asparagus, eggs or spinach. Below are some other derivatives together with their recommended partners.

BASIC HOLLANDAISE

A hollandaise sauce made using white wine vinegar.

MAKES APPROX. 300ML

Ingredients
6 tbsp white wine vinegar
8 egg yolks
2 tsp Dijon mustard
225g unsalted butter
salt and black pepper

• Place the wine vinegar in a small pan over a moderate heat and boil vigorously to reduce by two-thirds.

• Put the egg yolks and mustard in a food processor and blend for about a minute. Season well with salt and pepper.

• Melt the butter in a small pan and bring to the boil. Add the reduced vinegar to the butter.

• Slowly pour the hot butter mixture into the food processor with the blade running. Within a few moments the hollandaise will thicken ready to serve.

• Hollandaise should always be served warm. It can be stored in the fridge, but should then be reheated in a bowl over a pan of simmering hot water.

SAUCE BÉARNAISE

Recipe as for Basic Hollandaise, but cook a finely diced shallot in the vinegar and add some chopped chives, chervil and tarragon to the finished sauce. This is perfect with white fish, chicken or other fowl.

SAUCE DIJONNAISE

Recipe as above, but add an extra teaspoon of Dijon and 3 teaspoons of wholegrain mustard. This is the ideal companion for steak.

SAUCE CHORON

As Béarnaise, but add 2 teaspoons of tomato purée and some finely chopped sun-blushed tomato. This is a classic sauce to serve with fillet of lamb or beef.

THE OLD OVENS IN GUILDHALL

It was the first time I had been invited to cook in the mighty Guildhall and I clearly remember being shown around the huge back of house kitchen area. The Keeper of the Guildhall pointed out the two most enormous ovens I had ever set eyes on. These were massive iron structures, each larger than most modern kitchens with great cast-iron double doors opening to a blackened interior chamber. There was no floor to the ovens in order to provide enough oxygen to burn the five rows of giant gas jets. The only adjustment was a 'damper' at the top that would apparently, to some degree, vent and thus reduce the scorching temperature.

The Keeper proudly told me that this was where the Barons of Beef were cooked for the great City banquets and then added forcefully that I was not to go anywhere near them. I had my own private moment of pride when, some 10 years later, I cooked my first Baron for the 1994 Lord Mayor's Banquet in those self-same ovens.

WILD GARLIC OIL & OTHER INFUSED OILS

There is a lovely time in the early English spring when a steep shady bank of country lanes come alive with an abundance of wild garlic – first the leaves and later the delicate fragrant flowers. Every year this is a trigger point for enthusiastic chefs and restaurateurs as we gather bundles for both the Gladwin restaurants and Party Ingredients Catering. Wild garlic has a milder, fresher flavour than the root bulbs and can be frozen in small batches for use throughout the year.

WILD GARLIC OIL

A garlic-infused green oil.

MAKES APPROX. 500ML

Ingredients

500g young wild garlic leaves, well washed

500ml rapeseed oil

3 tsp salt

• Roughly chop the wild garlic leaves then blitz in a liquidizer or food processor into a purée.

• Warm the oil in a pan over a low heat, add the garlic purée and salt and cook for 5 minutes. Remove from the heat and leave to infuse.

• The oil will build in flavour over several days and can be stored in a squeezy bottle in the fridge for up to 2 weeks.

OTHER INFUSED OILS

These brightly coloured oils are a great way to glam up a plate of food. Experiment with using puréed yellow pepper and saffron; skinned and deseeded tomatoes with paprika; or tarragon and parsley. You will soon have a complete paint palette to add colour to finish your dishes.

A PRISONER IN THE TOWER

Among many noblemen charged with high treason and imprisoned in the Tower of London was King John the Good of France during the Hundred Years War.

While he was being held prisoner in 1360 he had with him an entire entourage – made up of a tailor, a secretary, a maître d'hôtel, a jester, various other attendants and even an organist.

In just one day King John was supplied with 12 chickens, a whole veal calf, 3 carcasses of mutton, 74 loaves of bread, 12 pounds of almonds, 8 sesters (whatever they may have been) and 21 gallons of wine. The prisoner even hosted King Edward and Queen Philippa at the Tower during his captivity.

HAZELNUT, JEREZ, CITRUS & OTHER DRESSINGS

Making a good dressing is as much about confidence as culinary technique. It is important to remember how little quantity is actually eaten and therefore the character of a dressing should be bold with contrasting combinations of savoury, sweet and sour. The chef's job is to taste and imagine – don't taste a dressing like a drink but taste with the finished dish in mind. This small section is to give your dressing-making skills a kick start. From here, the sky is the limit.

BASIC DRESSING

The basic ingredients of all the vinaigrette dressings.

MAKES APPROX. 250ML

Ingredients
200ml olive or rapeseed oil
40ml white wine vinegar
1 lemon, juice and zest
1 tsp Dijon mustard
1 tsp caster sugar
1 tsp salt
1/2 tsp black pepper

Equipment
stick blender

• Place all the ingredients into a bowl or open kitchen jug and emulsify together with a stick blender.

HAZELNUT DRESSING

Add 50g roasted hazelnuts and a little extra Dijon mustard to the above.

JEREZ DRESSING

Use sherry vinegar in place of white wine vinegar.

Use 2 tablespoons Fino sherry in place of the lemon.

Use 2 teaspoons of brown sugar in place of 1 teaspoon of caster sugar.

CITRUS DRESSING

Use the zest and juice of 1 lime in place of 1 lemon.

Use the zest only of 1 orange.

Reduce the white wine vinegar to 20ml.

OTHER ADDITIONS

Herb Dressing – add any fresh herbs you fancy.

Spiced Dressing – add chilli or other spices.

Honey Dressing – replace the sugar with honey. Add a pinch of cinnamon or lavender.

Create your own House Dressing – using other things.

'The qualities of an exceptional cook are akin to those of a successful tightrope walker: an abiding passion for the task, courage to go out on a limb and an impeccable sense of balance.'

Bryan Miller

WHITE BUTTER SAUCES

Another range of highly adaptable sauces are based around an emulsion of butter and cream. White Butter Sauce (Beurre Blanc in French) is good with almost any lean grilled meat, baked fish, or vegetables such as asparagus, mushrooms or globe artichokes. In this recipe we use tarragon and lemon juice, but try substituting these for fresh mint to go with lamb, or coriander and red chilli to go with seabass. Any herb can be used and other citrus such as grapefruit or lime juice can add a special zing to the sauce.

TARRAGON WHITE BUTTER SAUCE

The basic white butter sauce flavoured with herbs.

MAKES APPROX. 400ML

Ingredients

300ml crème fraîche

2 tbsp tarragon vinegar

2 tbsp freshly squeezed lemon juice

1 tsp caster sugar

75g unsalted butter, at room temperature is best

tarragon leaves, finely chopped

salt and black pepper

- Place the crème fraîche, vinegar, lemon juice and sugar in a small pan over a gentle heat.

- Cut the butter into small cubes, then place in a mixing bowl.

- Pour over the hot crème fraîche mixture, stirring constantly until all the butter has melted.

- Add the fresh tarragon. Season to taste with salt and pepper.

- Serve warm or reheat over a bain-marie, by setting the bowl over a pan of simmering water. Do this gently to avoid the sauce splitting.

SAFFRON WHITE BUTTER

Gram for gram, saffron is the most expensive commodity in the world. It comes from the tiny stigma of crocus flowers. Fortunately, we only use a very little at a time. The addition of a few strands of saffron to a white butter sauce will instantly provide an exotic, pungent floral flavour like no other.

VEGAN SATAY SAUCE

This is an incredibly useful recipe and is not just reserved for vegan guests. It is punchy, unusual and will enhance both meat and cooked vegetable-based dishes.

MAKES APPROX. 500ML

• Heat the oil in a pan over a moderate heat and cook the onion, garlic and chilli until lightly caramelized. Transfer the mixture to a food processor.

• Add the soy sauce, sugar, peanut butter and coconut milk. Blend to form a thick paste.

• Season to taste with salt and dried chilli powder.

• Transfer to a covered container and store in the fridge until ready to use.

Ingredients

4 tbsp rapeseed oil

1 onion, finely chopped

3 garlic cloves, finely chopped

1 red chilli, cored, deseeded and diced

2 tbsp tamarind gluten-free soy sauce

4 tsp light brown sugar

240ml peanut butter

240ml coconut milk

salt and dried chilli powder

A VEGAN DIET

In many respects a vegan diet is no different to any other. It needs the right balance of carbohydrates, protein and vitamins and needs to minimize free sugars. The main sources of good nourishment are fresh vegetables, fruits, nuts, seeds, calcium-fortified plant milks (such as almond yoghurt), cereals and grains. The chef's job is then to use this huge portfolio of ingredients to make exciting and delicious dishes. Our chef brigade does menu development focused on just this.

SAVOURY & SWEET SALSAS

The word salsa, simply meaning 'sauce', refers to mixtures of finely chopped or puréed moist, fresh ingredients, sometimes with the addition of oil. Salsas can be as varied, colourful and extreme as you like. Classics are tomato, green herb or chilli, but I would encourage any enthusiastic cook to be creative. A base such as aubergine, sweet peppers, pumpkin, avocado, watercress or tomatoes is a good starting point. An element of sweetness such as dates, sultanas or papaya works well. Nuts are also interesting and fresh herbs or unusual spices will make it special. Sweet salsas are good with desserts and there are examples of both below.

SALSA VERDE

The origins of salsa verde (green sauce) go back 2,000 years and I am sure there is a version for every one of those years. The anchovy gives a lovely salty flavoursome base, but this can of course be omitted to make the dish vegetarian.

MAKES APPROX. 200ML

Ingredients

50g canned anchovy fillets in olive oil, drained

5 tbsp olive oil

large bunch of flat-leaf parsley

bunch of sweet basil

1 tbsp red wine vinegar

2 tsp Dijon mustard

bunch of fennel tops or dill

25g gem capers

25g gherkins

25g pine nuts

salt and pepper

• Place the anchovies, oil, parsley and basil into a food processor and blitz to a purée. Add the vinegar, mustard and seasoning, then blitz again.

• Finely chop the fennel tops, capers, gherkins and pine nuts and stir these in. Season to taste with the salt and pepper.

'If an architect makes a mistake, he grows ivy to cover it. If a doctor makes a mistake, he covers it with soil. If a cook makes a mistake, he covers it with some sauce and says it is a new recipe.'

Paul Bocuse

PINEAPPLE, MINT & CHILLI SALSA

This dessert salsa can transform a dull pudding into something exotic and delicious.

SERVES 6

Ingredients

½ **fresh pineapple,** peeled, cored and finely diced

small bunch of mint, shredded

½ **red chilli,** cored, deseeded and cut into tiny slivers

1 **tbsp caster sugar**

• In a bowl, mix the pineapple, mint and chilli together with the sugar to taste and leave in the fridge to develop for at least 2 hours.

THE BIRTH OF THE STOCK EXCHANGE

In the late 17th century, stockbrokers and stock jobbers carried out their trade in coffee shops along Change Alley. Most notable of these was Jonathan Castaing, who issued a twice-weekly list of stock and commodity prices called 'The Course of the Exchange and Other Things'. Here is an extract from it:

London, Tuesday 4 January 1698

	Advanced	Paid Off
Tobacco	1500000	119400
Poll Tax	569293	479328
Salt Act	1904519	73772
Low Wines	69959	11100
Coal Act & Leath	564700	17162
Malt Act	200000	163745

By John Castaing, Broker, at his Office at Jonathan's Coffee House.

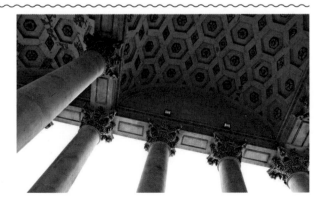

GOOD GRAVY

Why is it that so many keen amateur cooks work very hard to prepare nice food but then fail on the gravy? There is absolutely no need to use jarred or packet gravies. Techniques are easy, and natural flavours are so much more delicious. I have said in the section on dressings that it is all about confidence – for good gravy, my slogan is 'bravery and balance'! Be brave about adding great ingredients to boost the taste, but balance these carefully with one another to avoid drowning the flavours of the main dish.

TRADITIONAL GRAVY FOR ROAST MEATS

The fundamental requirements for good gravy.

SERVES 6

Ingredients

cooking juices from a roasted joint or bird

1 tbsp plain flour

500ml water, saved from cooking the vegetables or stock

200ml white or red wine

salt and pepper

Optional extras

These include garlic, shallots, wine vinegar, brown sugar, a little mustard, lemon juice.

Lamb – rosemary, thyme, mint sauce, redcurrant jelly.

Beef – horseradish, dried mushrooms, English mustard, Worcestershire sauce.

Chicken – tarragon, sage, honey, citrus zest, wholegrain mustard.

Game – mixed spice, treacle, quince jelly, cranberry, sherry vinegar.

• When the meat is cooked, transfer it to another dish to rest and cover with foil to keep warm. Place the roasting tin on a high heat on the hob.

• Bring the cooking juices to the boil (add garlic or shallot if you are using them) and cook for 1–2 minutes. Stir in the flour and cook for 1 minute. Add the vegetable water and wine, season well and bring back to the boil.

• Taste, add other ingredients and taste again until you are satisfied with the flavour. Please don't add all of my suggested additions – that would not be pleasant.

• Continue to boil the liquid rapidly to reduce.

• Finally, add any juices that have come out of the meat while it was resting, just before you serve.

JUS & REDUCTIONS

These refer to sauces that are not thickened with starch. The above instructions and additions can still be applied but with the omission of the flour. The jus may need to be reduced further to thicken and should be put through a fine sieve before serving. Where there is not a roast meat to use as a starting point, a good stock is needed. It is worth getting in the habit of making stock each time you cook a larger piece of meat by boiling the bones or carcass with onion, carrot, celery and garden herbs. Then freeze small containers of the stock for future sauces.

'I cook with wine. Sometimes I even add it to the food.'
W.C. Fields

CREAM CUSTARD & THE CITY

Think heaven and earth, dustpan and brush or bride and groom – words that always go together. Our traditional perception of desserts in the City of London is anything with custard. Spotted dick, treacle sponge, bread and butter pudding or even stewed rhubarb – the next word is always custard. There are, of course, custards and custards. A thin but rich Crème Anglaise is the most delicious thing while something bright yellow, thick and lumpy is one to avoid. Here is a good base recipe and then some guidance for variations.

CREAM CUSTARD

It all starts with a good base custard recipe.

MAKES 600ml

Ingredients

3 egg yolks

3 tbsp golden caster sugar

400ml milk

100ml cream

½ tsp vanilla essence

Custard additions

2 tbsp elderflower cordial, added when the mixture is thickening.

20ml orange blossom flower water and grated zest of an orange, added when the mixture is thickening.

Grated nutmeg or powdered cinnamon, sprinkled on top of the finished custard.

For a thicker consistency, a tablespoon of cornflower, added to the sugar and egg mixture at the start.

• Place the egg yolks and sugar into a bowl and blend together with a hand whisk.

• Heat the milk, cream and vanilla essence in a small pan over a low heat. Bring up to scalding point.

• While whisking the egg and sugar, slowly pour in the hot milk mixture.

• Return the whole mixture to the pan and put back over the gentle heat. Stir constantly while the mixture thickens.

• Remove from the heat just before it starts to simmer and transfer to a jug to serve.

• Alternatively, the custard can be cooled then reheated over a bain-marie (a heatproof bowl set over a pan of gently simmering water).

SOMETIMES THINGS DO GO WRONG

My wife of 38 years is an artist in both the kitchen and on canvas but she is the first to admit that she was not cut out for catering. In the early years, when it was all hands to the pump, she was roped in to help with a formal corporate Christmas dinner. Carrying a huge fully roasted turkey upstairs from the kitchens to the dining room, Bridget somehow managed to drop the bird and, to her horror, see it roll back down. There was no alternative but to dust it off, present and serve it with as much of a flourish as was possible. The guests were none the wiser.

The moral of the story is not to panic and always make the best of things. Also, don't enrol your family and friends in your work.

DESSERTS

PARTY INGREDIENTS' ICE CREAMS

There is a whole world of delicious Party Ingredients' ice creams just waiting to be explored in your kitchen. The flavours can be as exotic or innovative as you wish, but the technique is quite simple and does not involve ice-cream machines, churns or even repeated whisking to and from the freezer. Each recipe here makes 1 litre of ice cream.

BASIC LEMON ICE CREAM

Ingredients
6 egg yolks
225g caster sugar
100ml milk
300ml double cream
2 lemons, zest and juice

Equipment *(for all the ice creams)*
stand mixer

• Place the egg yolks and sugar in a stand mixer and beat until the mixture becomes pale and doubles in volume.

• Put the milk in a small pan over a moderate heat and 'scald', but don't boil. Slowly pour the hot milk into the egg mixture with the mixer still running and continue to beat for 5 minutes.

• Whisk the cream and lemon in a separate bowl until stiff but not 'dry'. Fold the cream into the egg mixture using a metal spoon.

• Transfer to a dish or plastic container and freeze overnight.

PRALINE & CHOCOLATE CHIP ICE CREAM

Ingredients
100g caster sugar (for praline)
100g whole sweet almonds
6 egg yolks
180g caster sugar (for ice cream)
100ml milk
300ml double cream
100g dark chocolate chips

• To make the praline, put the sugar and almonds into a small heavy-based pan over a low heat.

• Stirring occasionally, allow the sugar to melt, then boil until it turns to a nutty brown colour.

• Line a tin with baking paper. Pour the mixture into the tin and leave to set.

• Break the praline into pieces and chop in a food processor.

• Follow the Basic Lemon Ice Cream recipe, but reduce to 180g sugar and omit the lemon – instead folding the praline and chocolate chips into the whipped cream.

RASPBERRY & PASSION FRUIT RIPPLE ICE CREAM

Follow the recipe for Basic Lemon Ice Cream, but after adding the whipped cream, fold 100ml ripples of raspberry purée (not juice) and the seeds and fruit of four passion fruits through the mixture without over-stirring it.

REDUCED-CALORIE ICE CREAM

Follow the recipe for Basic Lemon Ice Cream, but reduce the caster sugar to 180g and use 150ml of natural yoghurt and 150ml of double cream in place of the 300ml of double cream.

MASCARPONE & HONEYCOMB ICE CREAM

Follow the recipe for Basic Lemon Ice Cream, but mix 100g of mascarpone with 200ml of double cream in place of the 300ml of double cream. After folding the whipped mascarpone and cream into the egg mixture, stir in 100g of Honeycomb pieces (see page 231).

OTHER ICE CREAMS

The sky's the limit...

'Ice cream is exquisite.
What a pity it isn't illegal.'
Voltaire

POOR KNIGHTS OF WINDSOR

Over a number of years I have been lucky enough to occasionally cook at Windsor Castle. The Medieval Great Kitchen is undoubtedly the most impressive culinary haven that I have ever seen. It is a very high vaulted 'hall' with skylights above, lined with beautifully polished copper pans. All the old wood-fired roasting ovens and ranges are still in place but have been seamlessly converted for modern banquet cooking. The Poor Knights were the 14th-century military knights of Windsor, impoverished from their wars in France and then 'pensioned' at the castle. The history of their dessert is not clear, but presumably the knights had a liking for sweet 'eggy bread' or French toast as it is often called. In this recipe we serve the Poor Knights with a kissel of red berries.

SERVES 6

Ingredients

4 eggs

¹/₂ tsp salt

black pepper

¹/₂ tsp ground cinnamon

300ml milk

2 tbsp brown sugar

6 slices of stale bread, cut into halves

60g butter

For the kissel

600g mixed berries

50ml water or red wine

1 tbsp caster sugar

2 tsp arrowroot

To serve

200ml crème frâiche

icing sugar

maple syrup

mint leaves

• Crack the eggs into a shallow dish, then whisk in the salt, a little pepper, cinnamon, milk and sugar.

• Dip each half slice of bread in the egg mixture, turning over.

• Melt the butter in a heavy non-stick frying pan over a moderate heat and fry the slices of bread on each side until golden brown to make the French toasts.

• Lift out of the pan onto a baking tray ready to reheat before serving.

• To prepare the kissel, finely dice two-thirds of the berries.

• Place the diced berries and water/wine and sugar in a pan over a gentle heat. Simmer for 5 minutes.

• Mix the arrowroot into a small amount of cold water in a cup. Make sure it is smooth then add this to the hot berry mixture and cook for a few moments until thickened.

• Add the remaining third of the berries and set the kissel aside to cool.

• When ready to serve, reheat the French toasts in the oven at 170°C/gas mark 5.

• Spoon the kissel onto the individual plates and add a good dollop of crème frâiche.

• Place the hot toast next to the kissel, dust with icing sugar and drizzle over maple syrup and add the mint. Serve immediately.

THE LOVING CUP CEREMONY

At the conclusion of a formal City dinner the Toast is, 'I drink to you in a loving cup and bid you all a hearty welcome.'

This is followed by a very obscure ceremony during which each guest at the dinner takes a turn to drink from large gold or silver chalices filled with spiced wine (the Loving Cup).

Three people stand, two face each other, bow, then while one removes the lid of the cup, holding it high in the air, the central person

drinks then wipes the cup with an attached napkin. The third, meanwhile, has his back to the drinker in order to protect him from unexpected attack while he imbibes (clear so far?). The protector then sits, the first drinker turns to protect, the lid man turns and takes his turn at the cup and the next person at the table stands to lift the lid. And so on around the tables until everyone has partaken. (I am told that the Distillers still use real daggers to protect the drinkers – so beware.)

STICKY TOFFEE SOUFFLÉ WITH GINGER PARKIN

It is assumed that 'City gentlemen' eat nursery puddings and, to be fair, a good proportion of them do. This, however, is a lighter and more sophisticated version of the family favourite, toffee pudding, but nonetheless it captures the essential indulgent 'stickiness' of the original. We are serving it with poached Victoria plums and a finger of Ginger Parkin, but the accompaniments are up to you – ginger ice cream would be good too.

SERVES 6 (LARGE RAMEKINS)

• Place the butter in a heavy-based pan over a moderate heat.

• Once melted, stir in the flour and cook for 1½ minutes. Keep stirring and slowly add the milk, making a smooth paste. Stir in the chopped dates, sugar and egg yolks, then remove from the heat.

• In a separate bowl, whisk the egg whites to soft peaks. When the date mixture has cooled down, fold in the whites.

• Brush the inside of the ramekins with melted butter then spoon in the mixture. Place the dishes in a deep ovenproof dish and pour in cold water around them to come halfway up the outside of the ramekins.

• Bake in a preheated oven at 180°C/gas mark 6 for approximately 25 minutes.

• To make the toffee sauce, melt the sugar in a heavy-bottomed pan over a low heat. Cook until it becomes a dark golden brown.

• Draw off the heat and add the water, standing well back as it will spit and splutter. Stir gently to combine.

• Cut the butter into small cubes and add to the sugar. Stir until dissolved. Allow to cool a little before finally adding the cream.

• While the soufflés are still warm, gently turn them out of the ramekins onto the palm of your hands. Either serve immediately or reheat in the oven when needed.

• To serve, arrange the plum quarters on individual plates. Pour a good quantity of warm toffee sauce in the centre and add a swirl around the edge.

• Place the hot soufflé in the centre of each plate. Dust with icing sugar, plum powder and finish with a finger of Ginger Parkin.

Ingredients

35g unsalted butter, plus extra for greasing

35g self-raising flour

240ml milk

85g dates, finely chopped

70g soft brown sugar

3 eggs, separated

For the toffee sauce

250g sugar

3 tbsp cold water

125g unsalted butter

140ml double cream

To finish

5 Victoria plums, quartered and lightly poached

sprinkling of icing sugar

sprinkling of plum powder

Ginger Parkin (see page 226)

ORIGINAL ETON MESS

One of the classic British summer desserts, Eton Mess originated at Eton College, Windsor, and is literally a 'mess' of mashed-up berries, meringue and cream. We served a more sophisticated version for the Queen Mother's official 100th birthday lunch hosted by the City of London on 27 June 2000. This is the recipe. The other story from that great occasion is that just before the toast, the Queen Mother turned to the Archbishop of Canterbury who was sitting next to her and said, 'I think you have taken my red wine.' I was buried in the kitchen so was not a witness, but it was reported in the press so must be true.

SERVES 6

Ingredients

3 egg whites

175g caster sugar

600g raspberries

1 tbsp icing sugar

450g strawberries

480ml double cream

3 tbsp kirsch

To garnish

redcurrants

baby mint

• To make the meringue, place the egg whites into a clean, dry bowl and whisk into stiff peaks. Continue whisking, adding the sugar a tablespoon at a time.

• Line a baking tray with baking parchment and dollop spoonfuls of the meringue mixture on to the tray.

• Bake the meringue in a low oven at 100°C/gas mark ½ for 2–3 hours. Turn off the oven and leave overnight for the meringue to dry out.

• For the raspberry coulis, blend 200g of the raspberries in a food processor, then push the mixture through a sieve to get rid of any pips. Add icing sugar until you are happy with the sweetness.

• Prepare individual plates with a 'necklace' of berries, using approximately 250g of the strawberries and 200g of the raspberries.

• Take the remaining 200g of the strawberries and chop into small pieces.

• In a large mixing bowl, whip the double cream with the kirsch until firm but not 'dry'.

• Fold the meringue, chopped strawberries and remaining raspberries into the cream.

• Spoon into the centre of each plate and decorate with the raspberry coulis, fresh redcurrants and baby mint. Serve immediately.

THE LORD MAYOR'S HONEY & TREACLE TART

It is generally known in the City who is destined to become the next Lord Mayor, but it is never certain until elected (the election of the Lord Mayor is a one-horse race held every September). Before the election the sole candidate is referred to as The Senior Alderman Below the Chair (SABC) and afterwards he or she becomes The Lord Mayor Elect. So I asked a certain SABC's wife – what was her husband's favourite pudding? Surely if you are going to become Lord Mayor of London you should be allowed to have the things that you love to eat at your inaugural banquet. This is what we came up with.

SERVES 8–10

• To make the pastry, mix the flour and salt together in a large bowl. Using your fingertips, rub butter into the flour until it is the consistency of breadcrumbs.

• Mix the egg yolks with the water in a cup. Pour this into a well in the flour and use your fingertips to knead the dough together into a ball. Wrap the pastry in clingfilm and chill in the fridge for at least 30 minutes.

• Grease the tart tin with butter. Roll out the pastry on a floured surface. Carefully fit it to the tart tin and neatly pinch off any excess around the edges.

• Prick the base of the pastry all over with a fork. Crumple a piece of baking paper so it will fit into the pastry case and fill it with baking beans or uncooked rice. This will prevent the pastry rising off the base of the tin when it cooks.

• Bake the pastry case in a preheated oven at 200°C/gas mark 7 for 10 minutes. Then remove the paper and baking beans and cook for a further 10 minutes.

• To make the filling, mix the honey, golden syrup, treacle, melted butter and double cream together. Beat the eggs in a separate bowl and stir them into the mixture together with the breadcrumbs, lemon juice and zest.

• Pour the filling into the tart tin, reduce the oven to 160°C/gas mark 4 and bake for 20–25 minutes until just set.

• While the tart is baking, make the streusel topping by rubbing all the ingredients together to form crumbs.

• Remove the tart from the oven, cover the top with the streusel and return to the oven for a further 15 minutes.

• We served the Lord Mayor's Treacle Tart with Passion Fruit Gel, homemade stem ginger ice cream, strips of stem ginger, a sprinkle of Raspberry Powder, mint (and even a drizzle of Mansion House honey on the top).

• At home it is quite delicious with just a dollop of Greek yoghurt or cream.

Ingredients

For the pastry

200g plain flour

pinch of salt

100g butter, diced, plus extra for greasing

2 egg yolks

1 tbsp water

For the filling

8 tbsp honey

6 tbsp golden syrup

4 tbsp black treacle

160g butter, melted

135ml double cream

3 eggs

80g fresh breadcrumbs

2 lemons, juice and zest

For the streusel topping

85g plain flour

1 tsp ground cinnamon

50g demerara sugar

50g butter

2 lemons, zest

To serve

40ml Passion Fruit Gel (see fruit gels, page 47)

300g stem ginger ice cream

20g stem ginger, cut into Julienne strips

Raspberry Powder (see page 45)

baby mint

Equipment

23cm loose-bottomed fluted tart tin

baking beans or rice

SOUR LEMON POSSET WITH ALMOND TUILE

This was the dessert we served for Peter Estlin (Lord Mayor of London 2018/19) at his own Lord Mayor's Banquet. He was looking for something simple, fresh and tangy to follow the Prime Minister's keynote speech to the City – and here it is.

SERVES 6 (IN SMALL CHINA DISHES OR GLASSES)

Ingredients

850ml double cream

250g caster sugar

4 lemons, juice and zest

To serve

250g carton raspberry sorbet

zest of lime and orange

edible viola flowers

Almond Tuiles (see page 228)

• Place the cream in a small pan over a low heat and bring to scalding point (not quite boiling). Add the sugar and stir until dissolved.

• Add the lemon zest and juice. Your mixture will thicken at this point.

• Pour into the dishes and put in the fridge to set.

• Serve the posset with a ball of good-quality raspberry sorbet on top, some citrus zest, an edible viola flower and an Almond Tuile.

A TRIUMPHANT DISASTER

In my youth as a budding star chef, I used to do regular public cookery demonstrations – to raise money for charity alongside a bit of self-promotion. My 'right-hand man' at these events was a talented young chef called Olivia Stewart Cox. Although hers was a non-speaking role, these demonstrations could not have happened without her.

At one particular demonstration we were performing on a stage under hot lights with close-up monitors to an audience of 300 people. I am no pastry chef at the best of times and foolishly I was showing how to make an almond and lemon tart. To the great amusement of the audience, the pastry was literally melting into strands in my hot sticky hands. Olivia stepped in and, as cool as a cucumber, rescued the dough, fitting it beautifully into the tart tin.

It was such good drama, some people were certain this was a put-up job; others simply wanted to know where they could find their own Olivia.

Toasts

The Queen

✳ ✳ ✳

Queen Elizabeth The Queen Mother

✳ ✳ ✳

The Lord Mayor
and
Corporation of London

MUSIC

The Band of the

Menu

Laurent-Perrier Brut

✳ ✳ ✳

Scottish Lobster with
English Asparagus
Puligny-Montrachet 1er Cru, 1997
Les Folatiéres, Domaine Henri Clerc

✳ ✳ ✳

Roast Saddle of Welsh Lamb
Jersey Royals
Carrots and French Beans
Château Léoville-Barton, 1988
2eme Cru, St Julien

✳ ✳ ✳

Eton Mess
Forster Ungeheuer Riesling
Beerenauslese, 1989

✳ ✳ ✳

Coffee
Petits Fours

CITY LANDS AND BRIDGE HOUSE ESTATES COMMITTEE

Chairman
Robin Anthony Eve

Deputy Chairman
Barbara Patricia Newman, CBE

Aldermen
The Lord Levene of Portsoken, KBE
David Howarth Seymour Howard
Gavyn Farr Arthur
David William Brewer, CMG

Commoners
Richard Bruce Crosby Farthing
Peter Joseph Martinelli, Deputy
William Ian Baverstock Brooks
Anthony Colin Graves
Philip John Willoughby, JP, Deputy
John Arthur Frederick Taylor, TD
John Leslie Bird, CBE
John Hedley Spanner, TD
Richard Gordon Scriven, CBE, JP
Christopher Robert Mitchell, Deputy
Michael Henderson-Begg
George Marr Flemington Gillon
Keith Allen Sargant
John Alfred Barker, Deputy
Stephanie Ella Maureen Currie, Deputy
Michael Robin Castle Sherlock
Benson Franklyn Catt, JP
Anthony Noel Eskenzi, Deputy
Simon Walsh (now an Alderman)
Jonathan Philip Charkham
Janet Owen
Dennis Cotgrove
Geoffrey Clive Henry Lawson
Ivy Margaret Sharp, Deputy
Anthony David Moss
William Barrie Fraser
Pauline Ann Halliday, Sheriff
Michael John Snyder, Deputy
Judith Mayhew

BANQUET

GUILDHALL
6th May 1995

MENU

Champagne

✳✳✳

Lobster of the Western Approaches
with a Julienne of English Asparagus
and Nasturtium Flowers
Stoneleigh Chardonnay 1993

✳✳✳

Escalope of Poached Atlantic Turbot
tied with Ribbons of Scottish Smoked Salmon
and Welsh Leek served with a Watercress Sauce

✳✳✳

Garden of England Sorbet

✳✳✳

Roast Beef of Old England
Yorkshire Pudding
Roast Jersey Royals
Carrot and Swede Purée
Runner Beans
Château Prieuré Lichine 1982
4 eme Cru Margaux

✳✳✳

Iced Soufflé of English Berries
Brown Brothers Orange Flora Muscat 1994

✳✳✳

Coffee
Petits Fours
Warres 1970
Delamaine 1963

TOASTS

HER MAJESTY THE QUEEN

✳✳✳

OTHER SOVEREIGNS AND
HEADS OF STATE
HERE REPRESENTED

✳✳✳

THE LORD MAYOR
AND CORPORATION OF LONDON

Music

**THE ORCHESTRA OF THE
HONOURABLE ARTILLERY COMPANY**
By permission of the Commanding Officer
Lt. Col. Simon Lalor, TD
Director of Music:
Major Roger Swift, LRAM, ARCM, LTCL

March	THE VALIANT YEARS	*Rodgers*
Selection	HIGH SOCIETY	*Porter*
March	COCKLESHELL HEROES	*Dunn*
Songs	LONDON AT WAR	*arr. Pryce*
Waltz	VOICES OF SPRING	*Strauss*
Selection	WAR YEARS	*Anon*
Feature	RUSSIAN DANCE	*Ferraris*
Selection	NEW SULLIVAN	*Sullivan*
Song	WE'LL MEET AGAIN	*arr. Pryce*
Selection	SOUTH PACIFIC	*Rodgers*
3 Soloists	POST HORN GALOP	*Koenig*

TRUMPETERS OF THE LIFE GUARDS
By permission of Col. Peter Rogers,
Lt. Col. Commanding Household Cavalry
Pipers of the 1st Battalion Scots Guards
plays a Selection of Pipe Tunes

Top: Menu from a luncheon to celebrate The Queen Mother's 100th Birthday on 27th June 2000.
Middle and right: Menus from The Banquet to commemorate the 50th anniversary of VE Day on 6th May 1995 in the presence of Her Majesty the Queen with 52 other Heads of State in attendance and 1,004 guests in total.

ST GEORGE'S RHUBARB & GINGER CHARLOTTE

I have tried to research the history of a Charlotte dessert. Some sources say that the dessert was created in honour of Alexander I of Russia. Others say that the dessert was originally named after Queen Charlotte, who was a great advocate of apples, and still others say it is a derivative of an old English word that means 'a dish of custard'. If you are none the wiser, don't worry: nor am I. All I can say is that we have been making these particular Charlottes in the City of London for many years and they have always been very well received. Where St George comes in – don't ask. I have simply added the dried St George's Cross of rhubarb to justify the name.

SERVES 6

- Cut the brioche into 18 thin slices. This is more easily done with either a slightly stale loaf or one that has been deep chilled in the freezer.

- Choose two pastry cutters: one that fits snugly into the bottom of the dariole moulds and the other that is the same diameter as the top. Cut six discs of each size out of six slices of the brioche.

- Cut the crusts of the remaining slices, then cut in half to get 24 half-pieces.

- To prepare the filling, place the rhubarb, apple, orange juice and caster sugar in a pan and heat gently over a low heat. Stir until soft. Strain the fruit through a sieve, saving the juice to finish the dish.

- Mix the orange zest, chopped ginger and egg yolk into the drained fruits.

- Melt the butter in a small pan over a moderate heat, brush the inside of the moulds, then spoon in some of the extra sugar for a sugar lining. Twist the mould so that it is completely coated, tip the excess sugar into the next mould and repeat until they are all sugar lined.

- Dip the smaller brioche discs in the melted butter and place butter-side down in the mould. Do the same with four pieces of brioche to line the sides.

- Fill the moulds with the rhubarb and apple mix.

- Finally, dip the larger discs in butter and place butter-side up to seal each mould.

- Bake in a preheated oven at 180°C/gas mark 6 for 20–25 minutes until crisp and golden.

- Turn out the Charlottes into individual dishes, pour Cream Custard around, and finish with rhubarb juice and a St George's Cross of dried rhubarb.

Ingredients

800g brioche loaf, slightly stale

500g rhubarb, cut into 2cm pieces

250g Bramley apples, peeled, cored and cut into 2cm cubes

1 orange, juice and zest

100g caster sugar, plus an extra 50g for dusting

2 pieces of stem ginger, finely diced

1 egg yolk

100g butter, for melting

To finish

Cream Custard (see page 168)

rhubarb juice

12 sticks of dried rhubarb

Equipment

6 dariole moulds

set of round pastry cutters

LAVENDER & HONEY CRÈME BRÛLÉE WITH CHOCOLATE FLORENTINE

A classic crème brûlée is hard to beat and remains a City and domestic favourite. In this version, we use the aromatic flavour of lavender but this can be replaced with peaches, raspberries, fresh mint, sweet spices or, of course, the original – vanilla pods.

SERVES 6 (SMALL DISHES)

Ingredients

500ml double cream

6 stalks of lavender flowers

6 egg yolks

40g caster sugar (for mix)

2 tbsp honey

40g caster sugar (for topping)

To finish

sprigs of lavender

6 White Chocolate Florentines
(see page 219)

• Place the cream and lavender flower stalks in a heavy-based pan over a moderate heat. Bring to scalding point (not quite boiling), then remove from the heat and leave the cream to infuse for 1 hour.

• Mix the egg yolks and sugar together in a large bowl. Reheat the cream, sieve out the lavender and stir into the egg mix. Add the honey.

• Prepare a bain-marie by setting the bowl over a pan of simmering water. Allow the mixture to thicken slowly for 15–20 minutes, stirring occasionally.

• Test the crème on the back of a wooden spoon – it should be thick and not run back together when parted.

• Pour into shallow dishes and leave to set in the fridge overnight.

• Cover the tops of the crème with a thin, even layer of sugar and place under a hot grill to melt, bubble and brown.

• Finish the brûlées with sprigs of lavender and a White Chocolate Florentine.

WHY SO MUCH HONEY?

The City of London is making a conscious effort to support the world bee population and there are now hives on the roof of St Paul's, the Lloyds building and Mansion House.

This quote is from the Heart of the City, a business-led City charity: 'Bees are critical pollinators. To throw out some statistics, bees pollinate 70 of the 100 crop species that feed 90 per cent of the entire world. But the problems wouldn't end there. A loss of bees would result in the loss of the plants that they pollinate; this would affect the animals that eat those plants, causing a chain reaction all the way up to us. You would soon notice the amount of fruit and veg available at your local supermarket cut by half and the world would quickly struggle to feed and maintain its 7.5 billion population.'

CHOCOLATE & HAZELNUT
BREAD & BUTTER PUDDING

I cannot even think about bread and butter pudding without the memory of knickers hanging across an ancient basement kitchen. It was in the early days of our catering when there was still an 'upstairs downstairs' etiquette in the City. A tyrannical beadle was in residence with an even more tyrannical wife in the role of housekeeper – the domain of Mr and Mrs Soft. The kitchen that we shared always had a washing line strung across it with the biggest knickers I have ever seen hanging out to dry. Why I remember cooking bread and butter pudding in these conditions I don't know, but please don't be put off the recipe – it is as delicious today as it was all those years ago.

SERVES 6

• Cut the crusts off the bread and cut into approximately 5mm thick slices – 10 slices of bread will be needed.

• Spread the slices with softened butter (keeping any left over to use later). Cut the buttered bread into quarters diagonally.

• Melt the chocolate with the cream in a bowl over a pan of simmering water.

• In a separate bowl, whisk the eggs and sugar until light and fluffy. Fold the melted chocolate mixture into the eggs. Stir in the whiskey and leftover butter.

• Grease a deep dish with butter. Spoon a layer of the chocolate mixture over the bottom of the buttered dish and then arrange half of the bread triangles on top in overlapping rows. Sprinkle with chopped hazelnuts.

• Cover with more of the chocolate and repeat the process with the remainder of the bread. Finish with any remaining chocolate mixture and hazelnuts.

• Press the bread down with a fork so that it is all coated in the chocolate mixture. Leave the pudding to stand for 4 hours.

• Bake the pudding in a preheated oven at 180°C/gas mark 6 for 30–35 minutes.

• Serve hot with Cream Custard.

Ingredients

1 loaf good-quality bread, preferably 1-day old

75g unsalted butter, softened

150g dark chocolate

425ml double cream

3 eggs

110g caster sugar

50ml Irish whiskey (I don't think they had that in the nursery)

50g chopped hazelnuts

To serve

Cream Custard (see page 168)

Equipment

18 x 23cm deep dish

'Your body is not a temple, it's an amusement park. Enjoy the ride.'
Anthony Bourdain

CHOCOLATE FONDANT WITH MADEIRA SYLLABUB

This is that over-the-top chocolate pudding, which, when you cut into it, oozes out a rich, runny centre. Your guests will think you are very skilled to achieve such a gourmet restaurant dish, but the truth is it is just a very rich chocolate cake served half raw.

SERVES 6

Ingredients

170g butter, plus extra for greasing

170g dark chocolate, broken into pieces

130g caster sugar

90g plain flour

20g cocoa, plus extra for dusting

1 tsp baking powder

3 whole eggs

2 egg yolks

For the syllabub

300ml double cream

2 tbsp runny honey

50ml Madeira

a pinch of cinnamon

1 lemon, juice and zest

Equipment

6 dariole moulds

• Melt the butter, chocolate and sugar in a bowl over a pan of simmering water, stirring all the time until completely melted and runny. Transfer to a mixing bowl.

• Sieve together the flour, cocoa and baking powder and fold into the chocolate mixture.

• Stir in the eggs and extra egg yolks – the mixture should be shiny and smooth.

• Butter and dust the six moulds with cocoa then spoon in the chocolate mixture.

• Bake in a preheated oven at 200°C/gas mark 7 for 7 minutes (precisely!).

• Make the syllabub by simply whisking the double cream in a bowl until it is stiff then folding in the honey, Madeira, cinnamon and lemon juice.

• Remove the fondants from the oven. When they are cool enough to handle, turn them out onto individual plates.

• Serve immediately with the syllabub dolloped alongside, garnished with strips of lemon zest.

NO RULES TO DESSERT WINES

Try berries with bubbles; sticky Sauternes with pastries, tarts and cakes; and rich Tokaji, Pedro Ximénez or Black Muscat with chocolate. But in reality it is whatever takes your fancy to drink with dessert.

Dawdle with a powerful red Shiraz while enjoying a traditional crumble; or cut the sweetness of ice cream with a flint dry white Viognier; or enhance summer fruits and meringue with a floral off-dry rosé. *Richard Gladwin, Restaurateur and Wine Blogger*

SANTIAGO TART WITH PEDRO XIMÉNEZ SHERRY

This is a very satisfying dessert to make. It is halfway between a tart and a cake, but has no pastry case or flour. It is absolutely delicious accompanied by a generous shot of Pedro Ximénez sherry.

SERVES 8

- Separate five of the eggs. Crack the remaining whole egg into the yolks and add 300g of the caster sugar along with lemon zest.

- Whisk together in an electric mixer until the sugar has dissolved and you have a thick batter. Beat in the almonds.

- In a separate bowl, whisk the egg whites to stiff peaks. Fold the whipped whites into the yolk and sugar mixture.

- Grease the tin and line with baking paper. Pour the mixture into the tin and bake in a preheated oven at 170°C/gas mark 5 for 45–50 minutes. It is ready when a skewer comes out relatively clean.

- While the cake is baking, make the syrup in a small pan.

- Bring to the boil over a moderate heat the remaining 100g of sugar, lemon juice, Pedro Ximénez and the rosemary sprigs, stirring occasionally.

- When the cake comes out of the oven, prick it all over with a skewer and pour over the syrup. Leave overnight to 'mature' before removing from the tin.

- Garnish the tart with segments of orange, grapefruit, pomegranate and baby mint.

Ingredients

6 large eggs

400g caster sugar

3 large lemons, juice and zest

300g ground almonds

50ml Pedro Ximénez sherry

3 sprigs of fresh rosemary

To garnish

segments of orange, grapefruit and pomegranate

baby mint

Equipment

20cm loose-bottomed fluted tart tin

ALMONDS

Wild almond trees, with their dark wood trunks and delicate spring blossoms, are very beautiful, but often bear very bitter nuts. Sweet almonds were one of the earliest fruit trees to be domesticated around 3,000BC in various regions of the Middle East, including Azerbaijan, Armenia and Syria. The trees were grafted and farmed because they are highly nutritious but also have health benefits. Almonds continue to be one of the most special and versatile ingredients used in a huge variety of ways all over the world.

WHITE CHOCOLATE CHEESECAKE WITH PERSIMMON & POMEGRANATE

Recipe contributed by Vic Annells, Executive Director, Central Criminal Court

I thought the very least I could expect from the director of the Central Criminal Court would be a steak and kidney pudding recipe together with recommendations of claret vintages to go with it. But apparently the dining at The Old Bailey has completely reformed. It is the Director's wife, Barbara, who has shared this delightful cheesecake recipe with us. I wonder if the judges get to eat it for lunch.

SERVES 8

Ingredients

250g digestive biscuits

100g dried dates, chopped

125g butter

600g cream cheese

200g plain yoghurt

2oz caster sugar

1/2 tsp vanilla essence

3 medium eggs, separated

400g double cream

300g white chocolate

2 leaves gelatine

sprinkling of praline
(see Ice Creams, page 172)

To serve

2 ripe persimmon, cored and diced

1/2 pomegranate, seeds removed from the shell

edible viola flowers, to garnish

Equipment

20cm spring-sided loose-bottomed cake tin

- Crush the biscuits into a mixing bowl and mix with the chopped dates.

- Melt the butter in a small pan over a moderate heat and combine with the biscuits. Line a cake tin with baking paper. Press the mixture into a cake into the tin to form an even base.

- Chill in the fridge for 30 minutes.

- Use an electric hand whisk to blend together the cream cheese, yoghurt, sugar, vanilla essence and egg yolks in a large bowl. Set aside.

- Place the double cream and pieces of white chocolate in a bowl over a pan of simmering water. Stir until the chocolate has completely melted.

- Soak the leaf gelatine in cold water for 10 minutes. Gently squeeze it out, then stir into the chocolate cream until dissolved. Set aside.

- Beat the egg whites in a bowl until stiff.

- Slowly beat the chocolate cream into the cream cheese mixture. When it is all mixed in, fold in the whipped egg whites.

- Pour onto the biscuit base and set in the fridge for 24 hours.

- Remove the cake from the tin, slice into wedges and dust with praline.

- Serve with the persimmon, pomegranate and an edible viola flower.

The Old Bailey, 17 April 1779

'Mary Owen… was indicted for the wilful murder of Henry Owen… or that she feloniously, traitorously, and wilfully, and of her malice afore-thought did mix and mingle a large quantity of deadly poison called arsenick, into a cake made of dough, which cake she caused and procured to be baked, and did give the said Henry the said cake to eat…'

CHEESE & SAVOURIES

APPLE PIE & LANCASHIRE CHEESE

The City of London loves tradition in all its forms. If we can justify a dish with some sort of heritage or an ancient folklore then it is an instant success on a menu, and the old Lancashire adage that 'Apple pie without cheese is like a kiss without a squeeze' is a classic. It is also very true that a rich crust, apple plate pie is the perfect partner for a mature English hard cheese.

SERVES 8

• To make the pastry, mix together the flour and salt in a large bowl. Rub the butter into the flour until it is the consistency of breadcrumbs and add the sugar.

• Mix the egg and water in a cup. Pour this into a well in the flour mixture and use your fingertips to kneed the dough into a ball.

• Wrap the pastry in clingfilm and chill in the fridge for at least 30 minutes.

• Turn the dough onto a floured work surface. Divide into two – one amount a little larger than the other. Lightly knead the dough balls then roll them out on a floured work surface.

• Fit the larger piece of pastry into a deep ovenproof pie plate, greased and lined with baking paper.

• Layer the sliced apples evenly across the pastry, coat with the brown sugar and sprinkle with the spices.

• Place the lid of pastry on top. Crimp the edge all round between your forefinger and thumb, cut off the edges, then use the offcuts to make decorative pastry leaves on the lid.

• Bake in a preheated oven at 180°C/gas mark 6 for 45 minutes.

• The Kiss with its Squeeze should be sliced into eight wedges. Add mature Cheddar, a teaspoon of quince jelly and a little sprig of fresh mint.

Ingredients

For the pastry

250g plain flour, sifted

1/2 tsp salt

120g butter, at room temperature

85g caster sugar

1 egg

1 tbsp water

For the filling

4 Bramley apples, cored and sliced

3 tbsp soft light brown sugar

1/2 tsp cinnamon

1/2 tsp ground cloves

To finish

400g mature Cheddar cheese, cut into fingers

quince jelly

mint sprigs

Equipment

26cm pie plate

Grace
God, who gave each man a stomach,
And a wife to comment on it,
Bless those who would desire us thinner,
Now let's eat a five-course dinner.
Amen

SUSSEX BLUE CHEESE PANNA COTTA WITH MULBERRIES

We created this dish in honour of the great English wine harvest of 2018. That wonderful summer gave vineyards in the UK the best quality and quantity of fruit ever known, and I hosted a harvest lunch in the City to celebrate. We served all things Sussex, including our new ferment of Bacchus wine. With it I made this unusual blue cheese panna cotta accompanied with grapes from the vineyard and mulberries from our garden. The result – something between a cheese course and a dessert. Make it at home with any soft blue cheese, grapes and choice of berries for the sauce.

SERVES 6

Ingredients

500ml double cream

120g Sussex Blue cheese, crumbled

2 leaves of bronze leaf gelatine

black pepper

oil, for oiling

For the berry syrup

100g caster sugar

100g frozen mulberries and their juices
(blackberries can be substituted)

To serve

250g fresh grapes, halved and deseeded

Equipment

6 dariole moulds, or similar

• Place the cream in a heavy-bottomed pan over a gentle heat. Bring to a simmer, stir in the cheese and allow to melt completely.

• Season to taste with plenty of pepper.

• Soak the gelatine leaves in a bowl of cold water and allow them to soften for a few minutes.

• Remove the leaves from the water, squeeze out the excess water, then stir them into the warm cream mixture and allow to dissolve.

• Lightly oil the moulds, pour in the mixture and transfer to the fridge to set until completely firm.

• Meanwhile, to prepare the syrup, place the sugar in a small pan over a low heat to melt and then caramelize. Keep a watchful eye on it, but don't stir.

• When the sugar turns a dark brown and is just beginning to burn, remove from the heat and quickly stir in the berries and berry juice. Add a little cold water if it is too thick. Be careful, the mixture will splutter. Set aside and allow to cool.

• Turn out the panna cottas by dipping the moulds briefly in boiling water. Loosen around the edges with your fingers, then give a firm shake and allow the panna cottas to fall into the palm of your hand.

• Place on individual plates and serve with fresh grapes and complete with the berry syrup.

MULBERRY TREES IN THE CITY OF LONDON

The exquisite taste of mulberry is like no other and it reminds me of my early childhood in Africa where there was an abundance of mulberry trees. We are lucky enough to have a very old tree in the garden at Nutbourne from which we harvest the berries every year to make a limited amount of mulberry purée and syrup. As far as I know, mulberries are still not available commercially in this country so it is one of those rare and special ingredients.

There are a few mulberry trees in the City of London. If you stroll down Throgmorton Avenue, behind the steel railings you will see the Mulberry Garden of The Drapers' Company; or in the Walled Garden of the Girdlers' Hall in Basinghall Street there is a fine mulberry tree. Alas, I think you would have to have some very good connections to be permitted to harvest the berries of either of these trees.

COMTÉ, PUMPKIN & BROCCOLI CHOUX

Choux pastry is an excellent thing to master for savoury or sweet dishes. It is one of the great French culinary skills – versatile and satisfying to make. In this recipe we are using a savoury choux with a Comté cheese, pumpkin and broccoli filling, but the same pastry recipe and method can be used with fish, meat or other vegetable fillings. Made as a single large crown, the dish is called a gougère and works well as a supper dish.

SERVES 6

• Put the water and butter together into a medium-sized heavy-based pan over a high heat.

• Bring to the boil and when the mixture is bubbling up the pan, remove from the heat, shoot in the flour and quickly beat until smooth.

• Return to the heat and cook for 2 minutes, stirring constantly.

• Beat the eggs in a separate bowl, then stir them into the mixture.

• Cook for a further 2 minutes, then add the grated Parmesan, mustard and seasoning. Remove the pan from the heat.

• Transfer the choux mixture to a piping bag and pipe small blobs to form little crowns that are approximately 12cm in diameter onto a baking tray lined with baking paper. Set aside while you prepare the filling.

• Fill the pastry crowns with pieces of pumpkin, chunks of the Comté cheese and broccoli. Season to taste with black pepper.

• Bake in a preheated oven at 200°C/gas mark 7 for 25 minutes.

• Serve the savoury choux hot on scattered salad leaves.

Ingredients

For the choux pastry

150ml water

50g unsalted butter

70g plain flour

2 eggs

60g grated Parmesan

2 tsp Dijon mustard

salt and cayenne pepper

For the filling

200g pumpkin, peeled, deseeded and cut into chunks

200g broccoli florets

150g Comté cheese, cut into small chunks

black pepper

To serve

salad leaves

Equipment

piping set

'How can you govern a country that has 246 varieties of cheese?'
Charles de Gaulle

BAKED FIELD MUSHROOMS WITH STILTON

Baked mushrooms filled with melted cheese are such a simple and satisfying savoury course, I am surprised they are not served more frequently. They can be made using up old bits of cheese, avoiding the expense of buying an elaborate cheese board section, and they are the perfect way to finish up the red wine at a good dinner party.

SERVES 6

Ingredients
6 large black flat mushrooms
20g butter
6 tsp quince jelly (or similar)
120g Stilton cheese, crumbled
40g chopped hazelnuts
black pepper

To finish
salad leaves
sprig of redcurrants

To serve
toasted sourdough bread

• Peel the mushrooms and cut the stalks flat (always save these precious by-products to make your next stock or sauce).

• Place the mushrooms on a baking sheet and fill them with a knob of butter, spoonful of quince jelly and the cheese.

• Season with pepper and scatter with hazelnuts.

• Place in a preheated oven at 180°C/gas mark 6 for 10 minutes.

• Arrange with some salad leaves and garnish with redcurrants.

• Serve immediately with toasted sourdough bread.

LLOYDS OF LONDON

Edward Lloyd established a coffee house in Tower Street in 1686, where he encouraged a clientele of ship owners, captains, wealthy merchants and brokers so they could arrange insurance cover for their cargoes and vessels.

This establishment moved around the City, steadily building in status and eventually becoming the specialist Lloyds insurance institution, which to this day dominates the international insurance market.

WELSH RAREBIT ON TOASTED WALNUT BREAD

City Banquets often follow the long tradition of serving a savoury course at the end of a meal to accompany the port or finish off the red wine. This can be something spicy such as devilled kidneys, Scotch woodcock or soft roes, or it is something very cheesy like this classic Welsh rarebit.

SERVES 6

• Melt the butter in a small pan over a moderate heat. Stir in the flour and combine to make a roux. Continue to stir for 2 minutes while the flour cooks. Slowly add the milk and beer, stirring constantly to avoid any lumps.

• Once all the liquid is incorporated, you should have a smooth, thick paste.

• Stir in the grated cheese, eggs, mustard powder and Worcestershire sauce.

• Return to the heat for another minute then spread thickly onto toast, top with sliced tomato and place onto a baking sheet.

• At this stage the rarebit can be chilled ready to finish and serve later on.

• When ready to serve, pop under a preheated grill until the top bubbles and begins to brown.

• Cut the slices into two and serve the rarebit with a few salad leaves and a dollop of homemade chutney.

Ingredients

75g butter

75g plain flour

200ml milk

200ml strong traditional beer

400g Caerphilly cheese, grated

2 tsp dry mustard powder

1 tsp Worcestershire sauce

3 eggs, beaten

6 slices good walnut granary bread, toasted

2 plum tomatoes, sliced thinly

To serve

salad leaves

homemade chutney

QUAIL EGGS BENEDICT

When I started out as a party caterer in the early 1970s, dances and balls always ended with a very early morning breakfast. It was part of a bygone decadence that, having danced all night, breakfast should be served before guests made their way home – hard on the catering team but great fun. Sadly this practice has steadily died out and we don't really expect to make Eggs Benedict at 3am anymore, but this mini version with Parma ham works well as an after-dinner savoury. It can even be served at a more civilized time in the morning when people have woken from a good night's sleep.

SERVES 6

Ingredients

small brioche loaf

20g butter

6 slices Parma ham

100ml Basic Hollandaise
(see page 156)

6 quail eggs

black pepper

oil, for frying

Equipment

8cm round pastry cutter

• Cut the brioche into 15mm slices and toast on both sides.

• Use the 8cm round pastry cutter to cut an even round out of the middle of each toast. Discard the edges or make into breadcrumbs.

• Butter the toasts and place them on a flat baking tray.

• Put half a slice of Parma ham on each piece of toast then a large dollop of Basic Hollandaise on top. Set aside until ready to grill.

• Gently fry the quail eggs in a shallow non-stick frying pan over a low heat. It is easiest to cut the shells open with kitchen scissors to avoid breaking the yokes.

• Lift the eggs out of the pan and keep warm.

• Place the toasts under a hot grill until the Hollandaise bubbles and lightly browns.

• Top with a fried quail egg, add a twist of black pepper and serve immediately.

THE SHERIFFS' BREAKFAST

Since the 7th century, long before any Mayoralty or council, there was a Sheriff of London responsible for collecting taxes and imposing the King's justice. Since 1132, the citizens of the City have had the right to elect their own sheriff and late in the 19th century, this was increased to two. We still have two sheriffs elected in the City every year; among their responsibilities is to oversee the Old Bailey, where they reside for their year of office.

The celebration to start the sheriffs' year of office is called The Sheriffs' Breakfast – but rather like a wedding breakfast, it is in fact a lunch. The oldest record of a City breakfast we could find is that of Samuel Pepys in about 1660, when the assembled company partook in a sumptuous menu comprising such delicacies as mutton pottage, turkey pie, goose, pickled oysters and collar of brawn, all washed down with ale and a pot of chocolate.

MATURE CHEDDAR SOUFFLÉ

A traditional hot cheese soufflé served straight from the oven is the ultimate ending to a great meal. I must dedicate this recipe to Susie Robinson, who founded Party Ingredients with me in 1975. This was a long time ago, but sometimes it feels like only yesterday.

SERVES 6

• Melt the butter in a medium-sized pan over a moderate heat.

• Stir in the flour and cook for 2 minutes.

• Slowly add the milk, stirring all the time until the mixture is smooth and thickened.

• Season to taste with salt and pepper, cayenne and the mustard. Stir in the cheese.

• Remove the pan from the heat and stir in the egg yolks.

• Whisk the egg whites into stiff peaks. Fold half the whites into the cheese mixture then the second half, keeping the mixture as light and airy as possible. Spoon the mixture into the soufflé dish.

• The soufflé can then be kept in the fridge for up to 2 hours before baking.

• Bake in a preheated oven at 200°C/gas mark 7 for 30–35 minutes, until risen and golden. Serve immediately.

Ingredients

30g butter

30g plain flour

150ml milk

salt and black pepper

¹/₂ tsp cayenne pepper

1 tsp Dijon mustard

200g mature Cheddar cheese, grated

6 eggs, separated

Equipment

1 litre china soufflé dish

A PARTY INGREDIENTS' SOUFFLÉ FROM 1975

My catering business was launched in 1975 with little resource, very limited experience, but a great will to deliver something exceptional. My original business partner was Susie Robinson, and she gained a reputation for excellent hot soufflés that is still with us 45 years on. Emma Spofforth, pictured opposite, and to whom this book is dedicated, is now the superb Director of cooking at Party Ingredients. The classic recipe and oven setting are the same as Susie used; even Emma's pose in this picture was used by Susie to promote the business in the very early days. Both the tradition of soufflés and the commitment to excellence continues.

SCOTCH WOODCOCK

Even some of the more gourmet diners in the City have been fooled by seeing Scotch woodcock as the last course on a menu – 'what an unusual idea to serve a game bird at the end of a meal'. It is in fact a very traditional Victorian savoury course comprising of smooth scrambled eggs and anchovies on toast. These were served in the Houses of Parliament as a staple until after the Second World War when the fashion for Scotch woodcock faded out. Now, hopefully the fashion returns, but nothing about it will remind you of a Highland bird.

SERVES 6

Ingredients

50g butter

6 egg yolks

90ml double cream

salt and cayenne pepper

6 slices of sourdough bread

12 canned anchovy fillets, drained

To finish

fresh parsley, chopped

paprika

• Place a heatproof bowl over a pan of simmering water on a moderate heat.

• Melt 20g of butter in the bowl.

• In a separate bowl, whisk the egg yolks and double cream together, season to taste with salt and cayenne pepper, and pour into the heatproof bowl.

• Whisk gently, allowing the mixture to slowly heat through. At the same time, toast the bread then spread with the remaining butter (or better still, spread with the Whipped Anchovy Butter on page 43).

• Place two anchovy fillets on each slice of toast, cut into two and place on serving plates.

• Continue to whisk the egg mixture and when it has just thickened, but not set, spoon it onto the toast.

• Finish with a sprinkling of parsley and a scattering of paprika. Serve immediately.

PRAY SILENCE FOR THE LOYAL TOAST
The origins of 'toasting' to an assembled company is fascinating and the name does literally come from pieces of crispy grilled bread. In the 16th century it was customary to serve a piece of toasted bread in pots of wine or beer. 'Drinking a toast' then became the fashion, and any excuse would be used to down an alcoholic drink together with the soggy toast as a salute to persons present, persons absent, or events.

The Loyal Toast was, of course, to affirm allegiance to the monarch.

CHOCOLATES
&
SWEETMEATS

WHITE CHOCOLATE FLORENTINES

Why is it that when we have clearly eaten an 'ample sufficiency' (as my dad used to say), we can always make room for a delicious chocolate or sweetmeat at the end of a good meal? Florentines are those irresistible, nutty, chocolatey, sweetie things that we all understand are very bad for us, but – met with a universal 'rude to say no' – they quickly disappear.

MAKES 12 LARGE (OR 20 SMALL)

• Melt the butter in a small pan over a moderate heat. Add the sugar and golden syrup.

• Remove from the heat and add the almonds, mixed peel, cherries and flour. Stir to mix completely.

• Allow the mixture to cool a little then divide into even amounts and roll into balls in the palms of your hands.

• Gently flatten the balls and place in a baking tray lined with baking paper. They will spread, so leave plenty of space between each one.

• Bake in a preheated oven at 180°C/gas mark 6 for 8– 10 minutes until golden brown.

• Leave to cool for 3 minutes before lifting onto a wire rack.

• To melt the chocolate, break it into pieces over a bain-marie (a heatproof bowl set over a pan of gently simmering water).

• Turn the Florentines over and paint the underside with a generous layer of the melted chocolate using a pastry brush.

• Place back on the wire rack, chocolate-side up, until set.

Ingredients

50g butter

50g caster sugar

50g golden syrup

50g flaked almonds

75g mixed peel

50g glacé cherries, chopped

50g plain flour

175g white chocolate

ROYAL CONNECTIONS

The City has a great history of Royal connections. Its wealth and immense power in the 16th and 17th centuries was only tolerated because of the huge financial support the Corporation and Livery Companies gave to the monarchy. The Lord Mayor and Aldermen were a seat of government to rival Parliament and their opulent feasting was second to none. Today there is a long-established tradition of the City hosting major Royal occasions.

State Visits follow a particular protocol. The visiting president or monarch dines with the Queen at Buckingham Palace or Windsor one night and the City hosts a State Banquet at Guildhall the following. Naturally the Queen's choice of menu takes priority. There is then liaison with the Embassy on the likes and dislikes of the visiting VIP and a committee of tasters is appointed to select the perfect menu and wines.

CANDIED ORANGE PEEL IN BITTER CHOCOLATE

Candied orange peel is a very traditional sweetmeat – so very appropriate for our City of London cookbook. The word 'sweetmeat' itself conjures up a bygone age of butlers and footmen delivering ornate silver salvers of sweet delicacies for the delectation of the guests. Like many traditional recipes, the process for making candied peel is quite laborious, but there are no shortcuts and the consolation is that your kitchen will have a wonderful citrus aroma for days afterwards.

MAKES APPROX 60 STICKS

Ingredients

4 oranges

1 litre of water

500g caster sugar

1 cinnamon stick

6 star anise pods

200g 70% dark chocolate

• Score the oranges into four pieces from top to bottom and remove the peel with the pith still attached. Cut the peel into long strips, approximately 5mm wide.

• Place the peel in a pan, cover with cold water and bring to the boil, simmer for 5 minutes then drain the peel strips and discard the water.

• Repeat this process at least once more. The orange is tenderizing and the bitterness is being rinsed out.

• Return the orange peel to the pan and cover with water. Bring to the boil then reduce the heat and simmer for 40 minutes.

• Add the sugar and spices to make a syrup. Simmer for a further 30 minutes.

• Leave the peel in its syrup to soften overnight.

• The next day, return the pan to the boil and cook gently until all the liquid has evaporated and the peel is well coated. Do not stir, but occasionally just swirl the pan. Carefully remove the peel from the pan and place onto a wire rack.

• Place the rack on a roasting tin and bake in a very low oven (50°C) for 2–3 hours to dry out. The peel can now be stored in an airtight container – for months on end if you want.

• To coat with chocolate, break and melt the chocolate over a bain-marie (a heatproof bowl set over a pan of gently simmering water).

• Half-dip the candied peel in the melted chocolate and then lay on a baking tray lined with baking paper. Transfer to the fridge to set.

'I never do any television without chocolate. That's my motto and I live by it. Quite often I write the scripts and I make sure there are chocolate scenes. Actually I'm a bit of a chocolate tart and will eat anything. It's amazing I'm so slim.'
Dawn French

FRUIT SORBET CHOCOLATE PEARLS

This is such a sophisticated treat and yet so easy to accomplish. I am not going to ask you to make your own sorbet – there are many good ones on the market you can use. Choose your favourite flavours and contrasting colours – orange, blackcurrant, passion fruit, lemon and raspberry are all delicious with chocolate.

MAKES APPROX. 40 PEARLS

• Using the melon baller, scoop out approximately 20 round balls of each sorbet onto a baking tray lined with baking paper. Insert a cocktail stick into each and return them to the freezer to firm up for at least 2 hours.

• Make sure that the balls are hard before you attempt to dip them in melted chocolate.

• Prepare two bain-maries by setting two heatproof bowls over pans of gently simmering water over a low heat.

• Break each type of chocolate into two separate bowls, stirring gently until melted. Remove the bowls from the heat.

• Holding the sorbet balls by their sticks, dip the bottom half of each one into one of the melted chocolates to coat it.

• Arrange the chocolate balls back on a baking tray. Return them to the freezer.

• Serve as after-dinner chocolates or even in place of a dessert.

Ingredients

2 x 400g tubs of good-quality sorbet in different flavours

150g white chocolate

150g dark chocolate

Equipment

2cm melon baller

40 nice cocktail sticks

THE BISHOP OF LONDON'S BANANA BREAD

Sarah Mullally is the 133rd Bishop of London and the first female one. Although resident in the City, her diocese spans both the City of London and the Royal Borough of Westminster.

The bishop very kindly gave us a recipe for her son's banana bread but regrettably it arrived too late to be included and photographed for this book. So you will just have to wait for another fundraising volume of recipes or, of course, you could ask her for it yourself.

BISHOP
of
LONDON

AMOR VINCIT OMNIA

GINGER PARKIN

This delicious gingerbread comes from the north of England and has been around in different forms for centuries. Cut into small fingers, parkin makes an excellent 'bit on the side' accompaniment to enhance fruity desserts, but it works equally well as an after-dinner sweetmeat and is reputedly good for the digestion.

MAKES APPROX. 30 SMALL FINGERS

Ingredients

110g butter

110g golden syrup

110g black treacle

110g soft brown sugar

225g self-raising flour, sifted

2 tsp mixed spice

1 large egg, beaten

140ml milk

110g stem ginger, finely chopped

a little icing sugar, for dusting

a little oil, for oiling

Equipment

25 x 18cm baking tin

• Place the butter, syrup, treacle and sugar together in a heavy-based pan over a moderate heat and stir until melted.

• Transfer to a large mixing bowl. Fold in the flour and spice.

• Stir in the egg, milk and stem ginger and mix well (the mixture should resemble a runny batter).

• Pour the mixture into a baking tin, lined with baking paper and brushed with oil. Bake in a preheated oven at 180°C/gas mark 6 for 25–30 minutes until firm.

• Cut the parkin into small fingers, approximately 8 x 2cm, and dust with icing sugar.

Good Grace

At very formal dinners, Grace is often sung at the end to thank God for the meal. Not this one though!

God give us grace, so in this race

There isn't just one winner

But fat or thin, we all can win

And share this lovely dinner

Amen

ALMOND TUILES

These delicious, crispy, wafer-thin biscuits – or tuiles – are often served alongside posh desserts. They are very 'City' and are excellent served as a sophisticated little flavoursome crunch at the end of a good meal.

MAKES 20

Ingredients

white of 1 large egg

50g caster sugar

25g butter

25g plain flour

½ vanilla pod

50g flaked almonds

- Begin by making a meringue mix. In a mixing bowl, with an electric hand whisk, beat the egg whites to soft peaks. Continuing to beat, slowly add the sugar, a teaspoon at a time.

- Melt the butter in a small pan over a gentle heat.

- Split the vanilla pod lengthways and carefully scrape out the seeds from the husk. Add these to the butter. (Vanilla is extremely expensive, which is why we are being frugal with it; save the other half and the husk to use in other dishes.)

- Using a wooden spoon, add the vanilla butter into the meringue, then fold in the flour.

- Line two baking trays with baking paper and place a large tablespoon of the mixture onto one of the trays. Use a palette knife to gently spread it into a 10cm round – it does not have to be perfect.

- Sprinkle flaked almonds on top. When you have three or four tuiles ready, bake in a preheated oven at 200°C/gas mark 7 for 5 minutes, until golden with a light brown edge. You will only bake a few tuiles at a time, but one tray can be baking while you prepare the next.

- Remove from the oven, wait 1 minute then, using a palette knife, lift a tuile and place it over a rolling pin to form a lovely curve.

- Allow the tuile to go crisp, then transfer it onto a wire rack. Repeat the process until you have used all the mixture.

- Store in an airtight container to keep crisp, ready to serve.

DOUBLE CHOCOLATE PISTACHIO BROWNIES

Brownies should be crisp on the outside (but gooey in the middle), incredibly bad for your waistline and truly irresistible. These brownies are all of these.

MAKES 12

- Place the chocolate, butter and vanilla essence in a heavy-based pan over a low heat. Stir until melted.

- Add both the sugars and cook until these are fully incorporated.

- Transfer to a large bowl and stir in the beaten eggs. Sift the flour, baking powder and salt and fold into the mixture together with the pistachio nuts.

- Pour the mixture onto a baking tray, lined with baking paper and brushed with oil. Place in a preheated oven at 170°C/gas mark 5 for 30 minutes.

- Once cool, turn out the whole slab and cut into neat diamonds; this will inevitably give you a few offcuts – a chef's perk.

- Garnish the plate with redcurrants and finish with a sprinkle of icing sugar.

- Alternatively, store in an airtight container until needed.

Ingredients

250g dark chocolate

250g butter

1 tsp vanilla essence

280g soft brown sugar

280g caster sugar

5 eggs, beaten

280g plain flour

2 tsp baking powder

½ tsp salt

80g pistachio nuts

a little oil, for oiling

To finish

redcurrants, to garnish

a little icing sugar, for sprinkling

Equipment

18 x 25cm baking tray

'The two biggest sellers in any bookstore are the cookbooks and the diet books. The cookbooks tell you how to prepare the food and the diet books tell you how not to eat any of it.'
Andy Rooney

HONEYCOMB DIPPED IN DARK CHOCOLATE WITH VANILLA MASCARPONE

This recipe is exciting, it is skilled, and it has a hint of danger – but don't let that put you off! It takes only 10 minutes to have a go at making honeycomb and is well worth the effort when your family and friends are wowed by your expertise. Caramel boils at a higher temperature than water and could spatter onto your skin – so please be careful or wear thin gloves for your first attempt at making honeycomb.

MAKES 20–30 SMALL SHARDS

- Line the baking tray with baking paper, sticking it down with a little oil.

- Put the water, sugar, glucose and honey in a large, heavy-based pan over a low heat. Do not stir.

- Once the sugar has dissolved, increase the heat to moderate/high and, using a sugar thermometer, carefully monitor the temperature as it steadily rises. Have a balloon whisk and the bicarbonate of soda at the ready.

- Once the temperature reaches 145°C, remove the pan from the heat, add the bicarbonate of soda and whisk rapidly by hand for 20 seconds. The mixture will react like a volcano; it will increase in volume by eight times and bubble up in the pan.

- Wait for 30 seconds and, when the bubbling is less aggressive, carefully pour the mixture onto the prepared baking tray.

- Put aside to cool and set.

- Turn out the honeycomb and break into irregular shards.

- Put the dark chocolate into a heatproof bowl over a pan of simmering water.

- Stir until the chocolate has fully melted.

- Dip one half of each honeycomb piece into the melted chocolate. Place on a piece of baking paper, which can be stuck to a baking sheet with a little oil, to set the chocolate.

- Combine the mascarpone, honey and chopped tarragon.

- Spoon individual mascarpone bases onto a serving platter and place a honeycomb shard on each one.

Ingredients

For the honeycomb

400ml water

300g caster sugar

400g liquid glucose

200ml honey

80g bicarbonate of soda, sifted

a little oil, for sticking

To finish

400g dark chocolate, broken into small pieces

250g mascarpone

1 tsp runny honey

6 tarragon leaves, finely chopped

Equipment

sugar thermometer

20 x 30cm baking tray

'The chief enemy of creativity is good sense.'
Pablo Picasso

TREACLE TOFFEE

So let's make the last recipe in this book the one that started it all for me, many years ago...

...the anticipation, excitement and collaboration for a Bonfire Night party; the enjoyment of preparing for a special event, with each member of the family having their own assignment. My mother allowing me the great treat of helping make the treacle toffee – a sticky pan, a rich irresistible smell, breaking the slab into delicious, great, chewy chunks. It is my earliest memory of cooking – now over 60 years ago. Treacle toffee, also known as bonfire toffee or crack toffee, is a traditional sweet served at Halloween and Guy Fawkes' night. Alas, my mother's recipe is long lost but we have experimented and this works. Careful of your teeth!

MAKES 30 X 20CM TRAY

Ingredients

60g butter, plus extra for greasing

400g dark soft brown sugar

2 tbsp water

200g black treacle

100g golden syrup

¹/₂ tsp cream of tartar

1 tsp white wine vinegar

Equipment

sugar thermometer (optional)

30 x 25cm baking tin

• Place the butter in a large heavy-based pan over a low heat. Add the brown sugar and water, but do not stir.

• Once the sugar has fully dissolved, add all the other ingredients, turn up the heat, give it a stir and watch carefully.

• The mixture needs to cook for approximately 20 minutes, steadily rising in temperature. Stir occasionally but don't overdo it or the sugar can crystallize.

• Using a sugar thermometer, take the mixture up to 130°C.

• If you prefer, you can measure the temperature the old-fashioned way: have a jug of cold water next to the cooker and dribble a little of the mixture in; the strands of toffee will set instantly. When they are firm but still flexible, the toffee is ready.

• Remove from the heat immediately and pour the mixture into a baking tin, which should be lined with baking paper and greased with butter. Take great care; it is very hot and could instantly burn your skin.

• Set aside to cool and harden.

• Turn the toffee out of the tin onto a flat surface, peel off the paper and break into bite-sized chunks. You can use a rolling pin for this.

• Store in layers on baking paper in an airtight container to avoid the toffee pieces sticking together.

Why my mother let her small, adventurous but accident-prone child help make this I will never know, but look what it got me into.

COUNTY CATERING – FROM CASTLE GARDENS TO SOGGY MEADOWS

The story of my varied catering career is not complete. There is the other side of the tale featuring estate-reared lambs roasted over open fires; freshwater crayfish in local streams; produce plucked straight from the vegetable patch; and vans stuck in muddy fields.

Depending on the success of this book, there are more recipes, oddities and anecdotes to come.

ABOUT THE AUTHOR

Peter Gladwin is a prominent chef in the City of London. He started his catering career 45 years ago and has stayed at the forefront of glamorous entertaining ever since.

From a child learning to make treacle toffee, to the challenges of cooking for great banquets, his enthusiasm and drive for all things foodie has never faltered.

Peter's achievements within the hospitality industry have developed throughout his career. He has run one of London's most successful catering companies (Party Ingredients Catering Services); he has been a restaurateur with two much-acclaimed restaurant groups (the latest with his sons, Richard and Oliver); he has owned a wine import business; and, together with his wife Bridget and youngest son Gregory, he produces fine English wines and purebred livestock at their farms in West Sussex.

Peter has published three previous cookbooks in his own name, and one in partnership with his three sons. Food and drink have always been at the centre of his world. Through recipes, menus and culinary anecdotes, this book explores the best that the Square Mile has to offer and brings cooking in the City right up to the present day.

Other contributors

HRH, The Duchess of Cornwall

Theresa May, former Prime Minister

Sarah Mullally, The Bishop of London

Rick Stein, Restaurateur, Cookery Writer and Chef

Susie Robinson, Co-founder of Party Ingredients

Sir Donald Brydon, former Chairman of The Stock Exchange

Vic Annells, Director of The Central Criminal Courts

Fabrice Lasnon, Executive Chef at The Savoy

C.J. Jackson, Principal and Chief Executive of Billingsgate Seafood School

Henry Harris, Restaurateur and Chef

Sabrina Ghayour, Cookery Writer and Chef

Sir Terence Conran, Designer and Restaurateur

Stefan Pini, Executive Chef for The Fishmongers' Company

Oliver Gladwin, Executive Chef of Gladwin Brothers Restaurants

Richard Gladwin, Restaurateur and Wine Blogger

With thanks

As always with cookbooks this has been a collaborative effort with a lot of highly talented people involved. My grateful thanks go to:

Simon Wheeler – this book would not have been possible without his creative eye and superb photography.

Kate, who coordinated the project at Party Ingredients, and my co-directors there – Vicky, Tim and Emma – plus Yli Tafaj and all the chef team who worked tirelessly on trialling the dishes and producing them for photography.

Helen Esmonde from The Stationers' Company.

The publishing team from GMC – Jonathan, Dominique, Sarah and Michael – who have been so supportive, patient and creative in producing a book we can all be proud of.

Three Lord Mayors, each of whom have trusted me to prepare their Lord Mayor's Banquets, for their encouragement and support of the project.

The many contributors, Livery Companies and City institutions that have made time to contribute recipes and other material.

And finally to my wife Bridget, and my family, for putting up with my hours of writing and avoiding the washing up.

Useful websites

Apothecaries' Hall
www.apothecarieshall.com

Carpenters' Hall
www.carpentersco.com/carpenters-hall

Gladwin Brothers Restaurants
www.gladwinbrothers.com

Guildhall
www.guildhall.cityoflondon.gov.uk

Party Ingredients Catering Services
www.partyingredients.co.uk

Skinners' Hall
www.skinnershall.com

INDEX

agar-agar 46

aïoli, seaweed 130–131

allotment salad 78–79

almonds

  almond tuile 228

  cauliflower & Romanesco couscous 81

  green herb macarons with goat's cheese 26–27

  heritage tomato & date tartare with almond gazpacho 96–97

  Romesco sauce 40–41

  Santiago tart with Pedro Ximénez sherry 194–195

  sour lemon posset with almond tuile 182–183

  watercress & almond soup 59

anchovies

  baked cod & tapenade crust with soft polenta & peperonata 112–113

  Salsa Verde 164

  Scotch woodcock 214–215

  whipped anchovy butter 42–43

apples

  apple pie & Lancashire cheese 200–201

  duck liver parfait with spiced apple 74–75

  Harvy Scarvy Norfolk relish 50

  roasted monkfish in Ibérico ham 120–121

  St George's rhubarb & ginger Charlotte 186–187

apricots, Moroccan lamb with apricots, chickpeas, cumin & fennel seeds 142–143

arancini, wild mushroom 94–95

arborio rice

  poached chicken with mushrooms, leek & courgette flower 150–151

  wild herb, lemon & butternut risotto 106

  wild mushroom arancini 94–95

asparagus

  allotment salad 78–79

  asparagus spears with Szechuan peppercorns 29

  kitchen garden ensemble 56

aubergines

  Moroccan lamb with apricots, chickpeas, cumin & fennel seeds 142–143

parsnip, sweet potato & aubergine dauphinoise 86

avocados

  avocado & oriental vegetable summer rolls 90–91

  barbecued pork chops with avocado & walnut salsa 152–153

balsamic vinegar

  pearls 39

  reduction 38

basil

  green herb macarons with goat's cheese 26–27

  salmon steamed in basil leaves with borlotti bean salad 116–117

Béarnaise sauce 156

Béchamel sauce 126–127

beef

  fillet of Beef Wellington 134–135

  gravy 167

  steak & kidney pudding 136–137

beetroot

  allotment salad 78–79

  beetroot ravioli with broad beans & edamame pesto 70–71

  chargrilled courgette cannelloni with beetroot, orange & cobnuts 18–19

  loin of Highland venison with Tuscan wine & dark chocolate sauce 138–139

blinis, dill, with smoked salmon, crème fraîche & caviar 30–31

borlotti beans, salmon steamed in basil leaves with borlotti bean salad 116–117

bread & butter pudding 190–191

broad beans

  beetroot ravioli with broad beans & edamame pesto 70–71

  broad bean hummus kofte with lentils & tomato concasse 104–105

broccoli

  Comté, pumpkin & broccoli choux 204–205

  fermented broccoli, with carrot, radish & spring onion 53

brownies, double chocolate pistachio 229

butter, whipped anchovy 42–43

butternut squash

  butternut & thyme tarte tatin 22–23

  butternut squash with hazelnuts 44

  courgette & butternut squash ribbons 87

  wild herb, lemon & butternut risotto 106

cabbage

  partridge breasts & damson wrapped in king cabbage 148–149

  roasted monkfish in Ibérico ham 120–121

Caerphilly cheese, Welsh rarebit on toasted walnut bread 209

cannelloni, chargrilled courgette cannelloni with beetroot, orange & cobnuts 18–19

carrots

  carrot & orange purée 85

  fermented broccoli, with carrot, radish & spring onion 53

  loin of Highland venison with Tuscan wine & dark chocolate sauce 138–139

cauliflower

  cauliflower & Romanesco couscous 81

  loin of Highland venison with Tuscan wine & dark chocolate sauce 138–139

caviar, dill blinis with smoked salmon, crème fraîche & caviar 30–31

Charlotte, St George's rhubarb & ginger 186–187

Cheddar cheese

  apple pie & Lancashire cheese 200–201

  horseradish & rosemary scones with chanterelle mushrooms 28

  mature Cheddar soufflé 212–213

  smoked mozzarella soufflés 92–93

cheese

  apple pie & Lancashire cheese 200–201

  baked field mushrooms with stilton 208

chicory, red onion & goat's cheese tarte tatin 107

Comté, pumpkin & broccoli choux 204–205

filo tulips with Oxford Blue, elderberry & lesser celandine 32–33

green herb macarons with goat's cheese 26–27

horseradish & rosemary scones with chanterelle mushrooms 28

kitchen garden ensemble 56–57

mature Cheddar soufflé 212–213

Parmesan crisps 56

red quinoa, baby spinach, orange & feta salad 80

smoked mozzarella soufflés 92–93

Sussex Blue cheese panna cotta with mulberries 202–203

Welsh rarebit on toasted walnut bread 209

cheesecake, white chocolate, with persimmon & pomegranate 196–197

chervil

  Béarnaise sauce 156

  green herb macarons with goat's cheese 26–27

chicken

  gravy 167

  poached, with mushrooms, leek & courgette flower 150–151

chickpeas

  broad bean hummus kofte with lentils & tomato concasse 104–105

  Moroccan lamb with apricots, chickpeas, cumin & fennel seeds 142–143

  red pepper & chickpea pakoras with pea & mint purée 102–103

chicory

  chicory, red onion & goat's cheese tarte tatin 107

  stuffed courgette flowers with Romesco sauce 82–83

chilli, pineapple, & mint salsa 165

chocolate

  candied orange peel in bitter chocolate 220–221

  chocolate & hazelnut bread & butter pudding 190–191

chocolate fondant with Madeira
syllabub 192–193
double chocolate pistachio
brownies 229
fruit sorbet chocolate pearls
224–225
honeycomb dipped in dark
chocolate with vanilla
mascarpone 230–231
loin of Highland venison with
Tuscan wine & dark chocolate
sauce 138–139
praline & chocolate chip ice
cream 172
white chocolate cheesecake with
persimmon & pomegranate
196–197
white chocolate florentines
218–219
chorizo, roasted monkfish in Ibérico
ham 120–121
Choron sauce 156
choux pastry 204–205
citrus dressing 160
clams, Billingsgate seafood curry
118–119
cobnuts, chargrilled courgette
cannelloni with beetroot, orange
& cobnuts 18–19
cod, baked cod & tapenade crust
with soft polenta & peperonata
112–113
Comté cheese, pumpkin & broccoli
choux 204–205
courgettes
chargrilled courgette cannelloni
with beetroot, orange &
cobnuts 18–19
courgette & butternut squash
ribbons 87
grilled lamb brochettes with
pistachio, honey & warm
spices 140–141
kitchen garden ensemble 56–57
lobster thermidor 130–131
poached chicken with
mushrooms, leek & courgette
flower 150–151
stuffed courgette flowers with
Romesco sauce 82–83
couscous, cauliflower & Romanesco
81
crab
cakes 114–115
florentine 126–127
cranberries
cauliflower & Romanesco
couscous 81
leek tarte fine with cranberry
relish 100–101

cream cheese
chargrilled courgette cannelloni
with beetroot, orange &
cobnuts 18–19
olive bark tuiles with pesto &
heritage tomato 34–35
white chocolate cheesecake with
persimmon & pomegranate
196–197
crème brûlée, lavender & honey,
with chocolate florentine
188–189
crème fraîche
dill blinis with smoked salmon,
crème fraîche & caviar 30–31
Poor Knights of Windsor
174–175
tarragon white butter sauce 162
cucumbers
herb & floral jelly mat 46
London gin-cured trout with
tonic & lime gel 64–65
cumin, Moroccan lamb with apricots,
chickpeas, cumin & fennel seeds
142–143
curry, Billingsgate seafood 118–119
custard, cream 168–169

damsons, partridge breasts &
damson wrapped in king cabbage
148–149
dark soy sauce, reduction 38
dates
grilled lamb brochettes with
pistachio, honey & warm
spices 140–141
heritage tomato & date tartare
with almond gazpacho 96–97
sticky toffee soufflé with ginger
parkin 176–177
white chocolate cheesecake with
persimmon & pomegranate
196–197
dauphinoise, parsnip, sweet potato
& aubergine 86
Dijonnaise sauce 156
dressings 51, 160
duck liver parfait with spiced apple
74–75

edamame beans, beetroot ravioli
with broad beans & edamame
pesto 70–71
eggs
allotment salad 78–79
kitchen garden ensemble 56–57
quail Eggs Benedict 210–211
Scotch woodcock 214–215
elderberries
filo tulips with Oxford Blue,
elderberry & lesser celandine
32–33

guinea fowl with wood pigeon &
elderberries 144–145
emulsions 156, 162
Eton Mess 178–179

fennel
fennel & kumquat marmalade 52
fennel & watermelon granita
98–99
Moroccan lamb with apricots,
chickpeas, cumin & fennel
seeds 142–143
fermented broccoli, with carrot,
radish & spring onion 53
feta cheese
kitchen garden ensemble 56–57
red quinoa, baby spinach, orange
& feta salad 80
filo pastry tulips with Oxford Blue,
elderberry & lesser celandine
32–33
fish
baked cod & tapenade crust with
soft polenta & peperonata
112–113
Billingsgate seafood curry
118–119
crab florentine 126–127
dill blinis with smoked salmon,
crème fraîche & caviar 30–31
Fishmongers' Company turbot
114–115
HRH's fish pie 110–111
king scallops & samphire seafood
bisque 72–73
London gin-cured trout with
tonic & lime gel 64–65
mackerel & seabass terrine
66–67
Persian salt & spiced squid
128–129
roasted monkfish in Ibérico ham
120–121
salmon steamed in basil leaves
with borlotti bean salad
116–117
Salsa Verde 164
Scotch woodcock 214–215
spicy grilled oysters 124–125
whipped anchovy butter 42–43
fruit
gel 47
powders 45
garlic oil, wild 159
gazpacho, heritage tomato & date
tartare with almond 96–97
gels
fruit 47
savoury 47
tonic & lime 65
ginger parkin 226–227

gluten-free
avocado & oriental vegetable
summer rolls 90–91
red quinoa, baby spinach, orange
& feta salad 80
sweet potato rösti with crispy
pancetta 20–21
wild mushroom arancini 94–95
goat's cheese
chicory, red onion & goat's cheese
tarte tatin 107
green herb macarons with 26–27
gooseberries, rabbit bonbons with
red gooseberry compote 24–25
granita, fennel & watermelon 98–99
grapes
Sussex Blue cheese panna cotta
with mulberries 202–203
wood pigeon saltimbocca 62–63
gravy, traditional, for roast meats 167
Greek yoghurt, lamb shank pithivier
with za'atar yoghurt 60–61
guinea fowl with wood pigeon &
elderberries 144–145
gurnard, Billingsgate seafood curry
118–119

haddock, HRH's fish pie 110–111
hake, Billingsgate seafood curry
118–119
Harvy Scarvy Norfolk relish 50
hazelnuts
baked field mushrooms with
stilton 208
butternut squash with hazelnuts
44
chargrilled courgette cannelloni
with beetroot, orange &
cobnuts 18–19
chocolate & hazelnut bread &
butter pudding 190–191
dressing 160
forager's wild mushrooms with
hazelnuts 84
Hollandaise sauce 156
honey
dressing 160
grilled lamb brochettes with
pistachio, honey & warm
spices 140–141
lavender & honey crème brûlée
with chocolate florentine
188–189
Lord Mayor's honey & treacle tart
180–181
honeycomb
honeycomb dipped in dark
chocolate with vanilla
mascarpone 230–231
mascarpone & honeycomb ice
cream 173

horseradish & rosemary scones with chanterelle mushrooms 28
HRH's fish pie 110–111
Ibérico ham, roasted monkfish in 120–121
ice creams 172, 173
infused oils 159

jelly mat, herb & floral 46
jerez dressing 160
jus 167

kissels, Poor Knights of Windsor 174–175
kitchen garden ensemble 56–57
kiwi powder 45
kofte, broad bean hummus kofte with lentils & tomato concasse 104–105
kumquat & fennel marmalade 52

lamb
    gravy 167
    grilled lamb brochettes with pistachio, honey & warm spices 140–141
    lamb shank pithivier with za'atar yoghurt 60–61
    Moroccan lamb with apricots, chickpeas, cumin & fennel seeds 142–143
leeks
    kitchen garden ensemble 56–57
    leek ash 45
    leek tarte fine with cranberry relish 100–101
    poached chicken with mushrooms, leek & courgette flower 150–151
lemons
    ice cream 172
    lemon mayonnaise 51
    sour lemon posset with almond tuile 182–183
    wild herb, lemon & butternut risotto 106
lentils, broad bean hummus kofte with lentils & tomato concasse 104–105
lobster thermidor 130–131

macarons, green herb, with goat's cheese 26–27
mackerel & seabass terrine 66–67
mango
    mango powder 45
    pearls 39
marmalade, fennel & kumquat 52
mascarpone
    honeycomb dipped in dark chocolate with vanilla mascarpone 230–231

mascarpone & honeycomb ice cream 173
mayonnaise 51
melons
    fennel & watermelon granita 98–99
    melon & strawberry soup 58
mint
    pineapple, mint & chilli salsa 165
    red pepper & chickpea pakoras with pea & mint purée 102–103
monkfish, roasted, in Ibérico ham 120–121
mozzarella soufflé, smoked 92–93
mulberries, Sussex Blue cheese panna cotta with 202–203
mushrooms
    baked field mushrooms with stilton 208
    forager's wild mushrooms with hazelnuts 84
    horseradish & rosemary scones with chanterelle mushrooms 28
    mushroom duxelles 134–135
    mushroom powder 44
    poached chicken with mushrooms, leek & courgette flower 150–151
    wild mushroom arancini 94–95

olives
    baked cod & tapenade crust with soft polenta & peperonata 112–113
    olive bark tuiles with pesto & heritage tomato 34–35
    salmon steamed in basil leaves with borlotti bean salad 116–117
onions, chicory, red onion & goat's cheese tarte tatin 107
oranges
    candied orange peel in bitter chocolate 220–221
    carrot & orange purée 85
    chargrilled courgette cannelloni with beetroot, orange & cobnuts 18–19
    red quinoa, baby spinach, orange & feta salad 80
oriental vegetables, avocado & oriental vegetable summer rolls 90–91
Oxford Blue cheese, filo tulips with Oxford Blue, elderberry & lesser celandine 32–33
oysters, spicy grilled 124–125

pakoras, red pepper & chickpea pakoras with pea & mint purée 102–103
pancetta, sweet potato rösti with crispy pancetta 20–21
panna cotta, Sussex Blue cheese panna cotta with mulberries 202–203
parkin, ginger 226–227
Parma ham
    quail Eggs Benedict 210–211
    wood pigeon saltimbocca 62–63
Parmesan crisps 56
parsnip, sweet potato & aubergine dauphinoise 86
partridge breasts & damson wrapped in king cabbage 148–149
passion fruit & raspberry ripple ice cream 173
pasta, beetroot ravioli with broad beans & edamame pesto 70–71
pastry 181, 201
    choux 205
    shortcrust 107
    suet 137
pea & mint purée 102–103
peaches, barbecued pork chops with avocado & walnut salsa 152–153
pearls
    balsamic 39
    fruit sorbet chocolate 224–225
    mango 39
peperonata, baked cod & tapenade crust with soft polenta & peperonata 112–113
persimmon, white chocolate cheesecake with persimmon & pomegranate 196–197
pesto
    beetroot ravioli with broad beans & edamame pesto 70–71
    olive bark tuiles with pesto & heritage tomato 34–35
pies
    apple pie & Lancashire cheese 200–201
    HRH's fish pie 110–111
    lamb shank pithivier with za'atar yoghurt 60–61
pineapple, mint & chilli salsa 165
pistachios
    double chocolate pistachio brownies 229
    duck liver parfait with spiced apple 74–75
    grilled lamb brochettes with pistachio, honey & warm spices 140–141
plums, sticky toffee soufflé with ginger parkin 176–177

polenta, baked cod & tapenade crust with soft polenta & peperonata 112–113
pollock
    Billingsgate seafood curry 118–119
    HRH's fish pie 110–111
pomegranate
    grilled lamb brochettes with pistachio, honey & warm spices 140–141
    red quinoa, baby spinach, orange & feta salad 80–81
    white chocolate cheesecake with persimmon & pomegranate 196–197
Poor Knights of Windsor 174–175
pork chops, barbecued, with avocado & walnut salsa 152–153
potatoes
    Fishmongers' Company turbot 114–115
    HRH's fish pie 110–111
    sweet potato rösti with crispy pancetta 20–21
    watercress & almond soup 59
powders 44, 45
praline & chocolate chip ice cream 172
prawns
    Billingsgate seafood curry 118–119
    king scallops & samphire seafood bisque 72–73
pumpkin, Comté, pumpkin & broccoli choux 204–205
puy lentils, broad bean hummus kofte with lentils & tomato concasse 104–105

quail eggs
    Eggs Benedict 210–211
    kitchen garden ensemble 56–57
quinoa, red, baby spinach, orange & feta salad 80

rabbit bonbons with red gooseberry compote 24–25
radishes
    allotment salad 78–79
    fermented broccoli, with carrot, radish & spring onion 53
    lamb shank pithivier with za'atar yoghurt 60–61
raspberries
    Eton Mess 178–179
    raspberry & passion fruit ripple ice cream 173
    raspberry powder 45
red berries, Poor Knights of Windsor 174–175

red peppers
  baked cod & tapenade crust with soft polenta & peperonata 112–113
  Moroccan lamb with apricots, chickpeas, cumin & fennel seeds 142–143
  red pepper & chickpea pakoras with pea & mint purée 102–103
  Romesco sauce 40–41
redcurrants
  Eton Mess 178–179
  Harvy Scarvy Norfolk relish 50
reductions 38, 167
relish
  cranberry relish 100–101
  fermented broccoli, with carrot, radish & spring onion 53
  Harvy Scarvy Norfolk relish 50
rhubarb, St George's rhubarb & ginger Charlotte 186–187
risotto, wild herb, lemon & butternut 106
Romesco sauce 40–41
rosemary
  horseradish & rosemary scones with chanterelle mushrooms 28
  lamb shank pithivier with za'atar yoghurt 60–61
  Santiago tart with Pedro Ximénez sherry 194–195
rösti, sweet potato, with crispy pancetta 20–21

saffron white butter sauce 162
salmon
  dill blinis with smoked salmon, crème fraîche & caviar 30–31
  HRH's fish pie 110–111
  salmon steamed in basil leaves with borlotti bean salad 116–117
salsas
  avocado & walnut 152–153
  pineapple, mint & chilli 165
  Romesco sauce 40–41
  Salsa Verde 164
saltimbocca, wood pigeon 62–63
samphire, king scallops & samphire seafood bisque 72–73
Santiago tart with Pedro Ximénez sherry 194–195
satay sauce 163
sauces
  Béarnaise 156
  Béchamel 126–127
  dark chocolate 138–139
  Dijonnaise 156
  Hollandaise 156
  Romesco 40–41
  saffron white butter 162
  satay 163

tarragon white butter 162
tartar 51
toffee 176–177
vegan satay 163
scallops, king, & samphire seafood bisque 72–73
scones, horseradish & rosemary scones with chanterelle mushrooms 28
Scotch woodcock 214–215
seabass
  HRH's fish pie 110–111
  mackerel & seabass terrine 66–67
seaweed aïoli 130–131
shortcrust pastry 107
smoked haddock, HRH's fish pie 110–111
smoked salmon, dill blinis with smoked salmon, crème fraîche & caviar 30–31
snapdragon flowers, mackerel & seabass terrine 66–67
soufflés
  mature Cheddar soufflé 212–213
  smoked mozzarella soufflés 92–93
  sticky toffee soufflé with ginger parkin 176–177
soups
  heritage tomato & date tartare with almond gazpacho 96–97
  melon & strawberry 58
  watercress & almond 59
soy sauce, reduction 38
spinach, red quinoa, baby spinach, orange & feta salad 80
spring onions, fermented broccoli, with carrot, radish & spring onion 53
sprinkles 44–45
squash
  butternut & thyme tarte tatin 22–23
  butternut squash with hazelnuts 44
  courgette & butternut squash ribbons 87
  wild herb, lemon & butternut risotto 106
squid
  Billingsgate seafood curry 118–119
  Persian salt & spiced squid 128–129
steak & kidney pudding 136–137
stem ginger
  ginger parkin 226–227
  St George's rhubarb & ginger Charlotte 186–187
sticky toffee soufflé with ginger parkin 176–177

Stilton cheese, baked field mushrooms with 208
strawberries
  Eton Mess 178–179
  melon & strawberry soup 58
suet pastry 136–137
summer rolls, avocado & oriental vegetable summer rolls 90–91
Sussex Blue cheese panna cotta with mulberries 202–203
sweet peppers
  baked cod & tapenade crust with soft polenta & peperonata 112–113
  Moroccan lamb with apricots, chickpeas, cumin & fennel seeds 142–143
  red pepper & chickpea pakoras with pea & mint purée 102–103
  Romesco sauce 40–41
sweet potatoes
  Moroccan lamb with apricots, chickpeas, cumin & fennel seeds 142–143
  parsnip, sweet potato & aubergine dauphinoise 86
  sweet potato rösti with crispy pancetta 20–21
syllabubs, chocolate fondant with Madeira 192–193
Szechuan peppercorns, asparagus spears with 29

tapenade, baked cod & tapenade crust with soft polenta & peperonata 112–113
tarragon
  mayonnaise 51
  white butter sauce 162
tartar sauce 51
tarts
  butternut & thyme tarte tatin 22–23
  chicory, red onion & goat's cheese tarte tatin 107
  leek tarte fine with cranberry relish 100–101
  Lord Mayor's honey & treacle tart 180–181
  Santiago tart with Pedro Ximénez sherry 194–195
  terrine, mackerel & seabass 66–67
Thai basil, green herb macarons with goat's cheese 26–27
thousand island dressing 51
thyme & butternut tarte tatin 22–23
tomatoes
  allotment salad 78–79

baked cod & tapenade crust with soft polenta & peperonata 112–113
broad bean hummus kofte with lentils & tomato concasse 104–105
heritage tomato & date tartare with almond gazpacho 96–97
olive bark tuiles with pesto & heritage tomato 34–35
Romesco sauce 40–41
salmon steamed in basil leaves with borlotti bean salad 116–117
thousand island dressing 51
treacle
  Lord Mayor's honey & treacle tart 180–181
  treacle toffee 232–233
trout, London gin-cured, with tonic & lime gel 64–65
tuiles
  almond 228
  olive bark tuiles with pesto & heritage tomato 34–35
turbot, Fishmongers' Company 114–115

venison, loin of Highland, with Tuscan wine & dark chocolate sauce 138–139

walnut & avocado salsa 152–153
watercress & almond soup 59
Welsh rarebit on toasted walnut bread 209
white butter sauces 162
wild garlic oil 159
wild mushroom arancini 94–95
wood pigeon
  guinea fowl with wood pigeon & elderberries 144–145
  saltimbocca 62–63

yellow peppers, baked cod & tapenade crust with soft polenta & peperonata 112–113
yoghurt
  lamb shank pithivier with za'atar yoghurt 60–61
  reduced-calorie ice cream 173

za'atar
  lamb shank pithivier with za'atar yoghurt 60–61

To Emma Spofforth – the most dedicated and hardworking chef I have ever worked with, now Executive Chef/Director at Party Ingredients Catering Services.

First published 2019 by
Guild of Master Craftsman Publications Ltd
Castle Place, 166 High Street, Lewes,
East Sussex, BN7 1XU, UK

Text © Peter Gladwin, 2019
Copyright in the Work © GMC Publications Ltd, 2019

ISBN 978 1 78494 555 8

The right of Peter Gladwin to be identified as the author of this work has been asserted in accordance with the Copyright, Designs and Patents Act 1988, sections 77 and 78.

No part of this publication may be reproduced, stored in a retrieval system or transmitted in any form or by any means without the prior permission of the publisher and copyright owner.

This book is sold subject to the condition that all designs are copyright and are not for commercial reproduction without the permission of the designer and copyright owner.

While every effort has been made to obtain permission from the copyright holders for all material used in this book, the publishers will be pleased to hear from anyone who has not been appropriately acknowledged and to make the correction in future reprints.

The publishers and author can accept no legal responsibility for any consequences arising from the application of information, advice or instructions given in this publication.

A catalogue record for this book is available from the British Library.

Publisher Jonathan Bailey
Production Jim Bulley and Jo Pallett
Senior Project Editor Dominique Page
Editor Sarah Doughty
Designer Michael Whitehead
Photographer Simon Wheeler

Colour origination by GMC Reprographics
Printed and bound in Turkey

Note: Unless otherwise stated in the recipes, vegetables are assumed to be medium-sized, milk is whole, eggs are large free-range, oil is extra virgin olive oil and teaspoons/tablespoons are level. Oven temperatures are for gas ovens and fan-assisted electric ovens. All measurements are in metric but for imperial conversions please visit www.gmcbooks.com/conversions.

Picture credits
All photographs are by Simon Wheeler except the following: Amanda Vail: 6 (top right); Clive Totman: 6 (top left, top centre, bottom), 12–13, 78, 118, 127, 151, 222–223; Frederic Guillon: 32, 219; London Metropolitan Archives, City of London: 11, 185; The Clink Charity: 40; The Skinners' Company: 122 (top), 123 (centre left, top right, bottom).

To order a book, or to request a catalogue, contact:
GMC Publications Ltd,
Castle Place, 166 High Street,
Lewes, East Sussex, BN7 1XU,
United Kingdom
Tel: +44 (0) 1273 488005
www.gmcbooks.com